Framework Media

CM01583918

CHATHAM ... SCHOOL FOR BOYS

9

Channels

Media in English at 11-14

Peter Wall

(Chief Examiner GCSE media and widely-published author)

Peter Bennett

(English teacher and widely-published author)

Consultancy by Kim Kenny

(Key Stage 3 English Consultant)

Collins

Published by Harpercollins *Publishers* Limited
77-85 Fulham Palace Road
Hammersmith
London W6 8JB

www.**Collins**Education.com
On-line support for schools and colleges

©Peter Wall and Peter Bennett
First published 2003

ISBN 000 713450 9

Peter Wall and Peter Bennett assert their moral rights to be identified as the authors of this work.

All rights reserved. No part of this publication may be reproduced, stored in a retrieval system, or transmitted in any form or by any means, electronic, mechanical, photocopying, recording or otherwise, without the prior permission of the Publisher or a licence permitting restricted copying in the United Kingdom issued by the Copyright Licensing Agency Ltd, 90 Tottenham Court Rd, London W1T 4LP.

British Library Cataloguing in Publication Data

A catalogue record for this publication is available from the British Library.

Internal and cover design: Blue Pig Design
Commissioning Editors: Helen Clark and Isabelle Zahar
Project management and development: Lucy Hobbs
Edited by Lucy Hobbs and Mark Dudgeon
Permissions: Mark Dudgeon
Production: Katie Morris

The Publishers would like to thank Kim Kenny for her valuable comments on the material.

Printed by Scotprint, Haddington

Channels Literacy Framework Matching Grid

	Unit	Word Level	Sentence Level	Text Level Reading	Text Level Writing	Speaking and Listening
Year 7	1 Front Page News	14		8, 14		1
	2 Telling a Different Story			7, 10, 11, 14		
	3 News and Youth		*13a*, 14	3, 10		
	4 Reviewing Music		*13a*,	10, 13	15	
	5 Analysing Soap Opera			10, 11		6
	6 Writing Soap Operas			10	5	16
	7 Popular Game Shows			10		6, 8, 16
	8 Interactive TV			3, 11	10	
	9 Pop Promotion			*4*, 8	10	12
	10 Making Popstars			10, 11, 13	10	
	11 Love Lyrics			7, 8, 11, 14		
	12 Writing Song Lyrics			6, 11	8	
	13 Reading between Lines and Beyond Images			*4*, 8, 10, 11		
	14 The Language of Advertising		*13a*	10, 11	*1*, 8	
	15 Gender Representation in Advertising			10, 11	*1*, 11	
	16 Creating a Print Ad			10, 11		7, 12
Year 8	17 What Girls Want		9	2, 9	17	
	18 Magazine Launch		9		10	10
	19 Magazine Advice		9		10, 15	
	20 Specialist Magazine Reviews	12, 14	12		*1*	
	21 Bigstar.com	14		*3*, 8, 9		
	22 Attracting an Audience	14		*3*, 8, 9		
	23 Reviewing Films	14		6	14	
	24 Film Information			6, 8	16	
	25 Analysing Radio News	14		9		9
	26 Writing Radio News			8, 9	10	9
	27 Analysing Factual Radio			9	16	10
	28 Adapting for Radio			8, 9	8	
	29 Advertising on TV			*3*, 9	17	7
	30 Different Audiences			8, 9	*3*	10
	31 Analysing Storyboards			9	11	9
	32 Creating a TV Ad			7, 9	*3*	9
Year 9	33 Analysing Pre-school Comics			8, 9	9	
	34 Bob the Story Builder			8	4	4
	35 Pleasing Older Audiences			4, 8		4
	36 Programming for Older People			4, 8	1	
	37 Analysing TV Trailers	7		*3*, 4, 8		
	38 Devising a TV Trailer			8	12	10
	39 Celebrity Stories			4, 8	16	
	40 TV Listings Features			4, 8	7	
	41 Access All Areas			8	10	10
	42 Site and Sound		8	8	4	
	43 Copyright – Arguing For	7		12	2, 13	
	44 Copyright – Arguing Against				2, 14	2
	45 Analysing Radio Ads			8	4, 9	
	46 Devising a Radio Ad			8	4, 7	
	47 Brand New!			8	6, 7	
	48 Letters Eight-foot High			8	4, 12	

Objectives listed in *italics* are those which underpin many reading and writing tasks and are not specifically media objectives. These could be termed 'implicit' objectives.

FRAMEWORK MEDIA

Contents

Radio

Moving Image: Advertising

YEAR 9 MIXED MEDIA UNITS

Targetting Specific Audiences

Promotion v Information

The Music Industry

Advertising and Branding

SECTION 4: REFERENCE

KEY:

L = double-length units **IT** = Units focusing on new technologies **ER** = Units with necessary Extra Resources

Introduction

Increasingly the way in which we see both the world and ourselves is shaped by the media. It is important, therefore, that we try to understand just what the impact of the media is and how it is achieved. We hope that this book will enable your students to take the first steps towards this understanding.

How to Use this Book

Channels is an exciting new collection of media material meeting the requirements for media within English across Years 7, 8 and 9. It provides strong material in areas such as moving image and sound that is absent from many other media resources. *Channels* has been devised with the busy teacher in mind, requiring minimal additional resources, though it is hoped that the work will lead to extended activities using the very media that the book explores.

The book offers 16 units for each year of Key Stage 3, with media texts ranging from pop song lyrics and TV trailers to Glossy magazine ads and Internet home pages. The stimulus material that appears on the right-hand page of each unit, is analysed as an example of a particular text type and often used as a model for the student's own writing.

Units are devised around the four-part lesson structure recommended by the English Strategy, and the objectives of the *Framework for Teaching English*, each comprising Starter, Introduction, Development and Plenary activities. While it is envisaged that most units will be delivered in a 50-minute to one-hour lesson, there may be times when activities naturally extend into a second lesson. This will certainly be true for the two double-length units in each year grouping where the writing activities involve a fuller planning process and/or the stimulus material requires more detailed analysis. (See units marked **L** in the Contents list.)

Further opportunities for extending work beyond the unit are offered by the optional 'Extra Resources' listed at the start of some units. For example, by recording a clip from a TV programme an existing activity can be applied to a longer media text than is presented in the book.

TIME-SAVING LAYOUT

The organisation of each unit should prove invaluable in both planning and delivering media lessons that follow the four-part lesson structure of the *Framework for Teaching English* document.

whole class | in groups

in pairs | on your own

Class organisation icons indicate how students may be grouped for each activity. A unit usually begins with a whole class Starter and then branches off into group, pair work or individual work before returning for a class Plenary.

PC photocopy | OHT overhead tranparency

PC and OHT icons are used where it is appropriate for the class to annotate a stimulus text using a photocopy, or to display a text or students' writing on an OHT.

Lesson objectives are laid out at the start of each unit for discussion with the students.

Following on from this, the activity headings in each spread clearly signpost the four parts of the lesson.

Extra resources are outlined on spreads whenever there is a need for an additional media text to be supplied for an activity. These are detailed either as being Necessary or, more usually, Optional. (See Contents list for those units requiring extra resources **ER**.)

Information boxes feature on many spreads, providing explanations of key terms or further data for students to use alongside their analysis of the stimulus text.

Modelling of writing and example answers are included in every unit. They are signalled by the use of a handwriting font. As the modelling of writing is a method fundamental to the delivery of the *Framework for Teaching English*, it is important for students to have access to models in different text types on which to base their own writing.

Storyboard Skills are highlighted in a section on pages 116-119, which looks at different camera shots and movements. It contains a model storyboard for a breakfast cereal, which employs many of the camera techniques discussed. This section is referenced throughout the book wherever students consider storyboards, whether for a TV advertisement, a TV drama plot or a TV trailer.

A **Glossary** on pages 120-125 provides explanations of all the media terms used in the book, and in particular those highlighted as key terms in each unit.

The **Wordlog and Spellofax** templates on pages 126-127 offer students a chance to compile customised lists of the media terms that they want to remember and know how to spell.

Coverage of the Framework Objectives

In a book focussing on media within English it has been necessary to prioritise those objectives in the Framework which refer specifically to media-related outcomes. The matching grid at the front of the book summarises the coverage of these objectives for each unit.

However, this prioritisation has not been at the expense of other key objectives. The objectives highlighted in italics are what have been termed 'implicit' objectives, i.e. those that relate to skills which should run as constant threads through all good English lessons, such as structured discussion, active listening, note-taking and collaborative group work.

In terms of adherence to the four-part lesson, it should be noted that Starter activities do not always use word and sentence level objectives as their basis, although there is a clear focus on language in all lessons. Starters in this book take an integral approach to lessons i.e. they are linked to the content and direction of the sessions that follow them. For this reason, Starters are often based around relevant reading objectives.

By following the units in *Channels*, students will both cover the media objectives outlined in the *Framework for Teaching English* and gain a good grounding in media skills in the lead-up to GCSE.

01 Front Page News

OBJECTIVES W14, TR8, TR14, SL1

- **To define and deploy words with precision, including their exact implication in context**
- **To infer and deduce meanings using evidence in the text, identifying where and how meanings are implied**
- **To recognise how writers' language choices can enhance meaning, e.g. *repetition, emotive vocabulary, varied sentence structure or line length, sound effects***
- **To use talk as a tool for clarifying ideas e.g. by articulating problems, or asking pertinent questions**

In this lesson you will look at how words and pictures work together on the front page of a newspaper to create a range of meanings for the readers.

STARTER

Tabloids and Broadsheets

The word **tabloid** refers to the shape of a newspaper. The *Daily Express* is an example of tabloid format. The word **broadsheet** is used to refer to a larger shape of newspaper. The *Daily Telegraph* is an example of broadsheet format. Brainstorm examples of these two formats from the national press. Which format do you think is easier to read? Explain why.

The words tabloid and broadsheet are also used to describe differences in content, style and presentation between the two types of newspaper.

- Under the headings Tabloid and Broadsheet, write down what you would expect to find when looking at the front page of each. An example is modelled below.

Tabloid	Broadsheet
Celebrity Gossip	Main news item of the day

Extra Resources

Necessary: Development - several headlines from tabloid newspapers.

INTRODUCTION

Parts of a Newspaper Page

Here are six terms used to describe features of a newspaper page.

Explain what you think each term means and match it to an example from the front page opposite. The first has been done for you. Be prepared to share your ideas with the class.

1 By-line - a line of print telling us who wrote the article, e.g. (c)
2 Headline
3 Masthead
4 Photograph
5 Column
6 Lead story

Now think about the **purpose** of some of the features. Look again at the front page opposite, and answer these questions:

- Why does the headline stand out from the rest of the page? Consider word- and sentence-level features such as a play on words or repetition
- What do you see in the photograph? Why was it chosen?
- Why does the photograph not have a caption?
- What is the main story, or front page lead, about? Who wrote it?
- What does the first paragraph tell us? Does it make you want to read more of the story?

Feed back your responses to the class.

INFO

Headlines

Headlines are written by a sub-editor who must ensure that the words catch the readers' attention very quickly. They are written after a journalist has written the story.

DEVELOPMENT

Writing Headlines

Now take a look at the wording used in headlines. Working in pairs, look at two or three headlines from tabloids. Consider the following:

- What the headlines tell us about the story
- How they gain the reader's interest and with what types of words, e.g. verbs, adjectives

Imagine it is your job to write the headlines for a **tabloid**. Decide what would be a good headline for each of these stories.

- The Government has decided that the Queen should be replaced as Head of State by an elected president. Elections will take place in the next year.
- Scientists have with conclusive proof that there is a primitive life form on Mars, after analysing rock samples from the planet.
- Schoolchildren aged 11 to 16, who have behaved well in classes, are to receive a reward of £20 a week. Badly-behaved pupils will be required to remain in school all weekend to help with cleaning duties, the Education Secretary announced today.

PLENARY

OHT

Present your headlines to the class. It may help to present them on an OHT. Comment on headlines from other groups, identifying one point that was particularly effective and why you thought so.

Which visual and language features of the front page do you think most attract readers of a tabloid newspaper?

02 Telling a Different Story

OBJECTIVES TR7, TR10, TR11, TR14

- **To identify the main points, processes or ideas in a text and how they are sequenced and developed by the writer**
- **To identify how media texts are tailored to suit their audience, and recognise that audience responses vary, e.g. *popular websites***
- **To recognise how print, sounds and still or moving images combine to create meaning**
- **To recognise how writers' language choices can enhance meaning, e.g. *repetition, emotive vocabulary, varied sentence structure or line length, sound effects***

Extra Resources

Optional: Development - articles from a Tabloid and Broadsheet covering the same story.

In this lesson you will look at the different ways in which the same news story can be told in tabloid and broadsheet newspapers. This is called the angle or point of view in the story.

STARTER

Headline Differences

Look at the two articles on the opposite page. They both cover the same item of news, but each is from a different newspaper. One is from the front page of a **tabloid** newspaper, the other is from the front page of a **broadsheet.**

First examine the headlines and write down three ways in which they are different from each other. Consider both the visuals used and the language features of the headlines.

- What the words say and mean
- How the words are printed on the page
- Visuals: the photograph

Follow the model answer below.

The tabloid headline describes the storm as a person, a killer and uses numbers to give the 'angle' a factual impression. It uses powerful verbs like 'crushed' and 'die' whereas the broadsheet uses less emotive language. Instead it uses exaggeration by saying 'leaves a trail of death and destruction as if it were part of a war that has not ended.

The tabloid fills most of the page with a mid shot of the effects of the storm. The broadsheet relies on telling the story with a longer headline and does not include a photograph.

INTRODUCTION

Story Differences

Now look at the articles as a whole and discuss the following questions. One story has an illustration in the form of a photograph. The other does not.

- Why do you think the editor of the tabloid paper has chosen to use a photograph?
- What is the photograph re-presenting to the reader?
- Do you think the photograph tells us anything that is not already covered in the story?
- How does the photograph link or contrast with the story?
- What 'angle' or point of view is the story taking? Try to give examples from the text in your answer.
- What do you think the photograph and the layout tell us about the way the *Daily Mirror* likes to 'speak' to its audience?

DEVELOPMENT

Choice of Language and Style

Having looked closely at the headlines, now look in detail at the main story text of the two articles. Using the headings below, write a detailed analysis explaining *how* the two newspapers re-present the *same* story in different ways

Note: analyse only the first two paragraphs of the *Daily Telegraph* but all of the *Daily Mirror* text.

- 'Facts' e.g. numbers of dead, location etc.
- Structure of the paragraphs, i.e. they answer the questions Who, What, Where, When and How

DAILY Mirror

NEWSPAPER OF THE YEAR

REVEALED: The TEN most irritating people in Britain

3AM SPECIAL: PAGES 12&13

3 CHILDREN CRUSHED AS 8 DIE IN GALES

KILLER STORM

By PAUL BYRNE and STEPHEN WHITE

EIGHT people, including three children, died yesterday in the fierce storms that battered Britain.

Winds gusting up to nearly 100mph caused chaos across the country and an estimated £50million worth of damage.

Two young boys were killed by falling trees. A girl of 14 died when a tree crashed down on to her family's car.

A lucky mother and daughter escaped from this car seconds before it was crushed by a falling tree. Diane Chauley and daughter Louisa, fled from their VW Polo as gales lashed the Bristol area.

Across the country rail, air and sea travel were badly hit.

Buildings were damaged and thousands of homes were without electricity after power cables were brought down.

FULL STORY: PAGES 4&5

READ ... ELLER EVERY DAY

The Daily Telegraph

www.telegraph.co.uk

BRITAIN'S BEST-SELLING QUALITY DAILY

Monday, October 28, 2002 FINAL No. 45,971 55p

Storm-force winds leave trail of death and destruction

BY NEIL TWEEDIE AND NICOLE MARTIN

Seven people, among them three children, were killed yesterday as storm-force winds brought chaos to much of Britain.

Airports and roads were closed, ferry services suspended and power supplies to more than 100,000 homes cut as winds of up to 96mph battered the country, causing damage of at least £50 million.

Three of the victims were killed in separate incidents in East Anglia yesterday morning.

Christopher Vince, 12, died from head injuries after he and his dog were crushed by an uprooted tree while walking in woods with his family near the village of Costessey in Norfolk.

... pushchair when he was hit by a falling tree. His mother drove him to hospital, but he was pronounced dead from head injuries.

Eric White, 55, was the third victim in East Anglia. He died after being struck by a falling tree in the garden of his home in Whittington, Norfolk.

In Shropshire, an 11-year-old girl was killed and her mother and sister seriously injured when their car was hit by a flying branch on the A41 near Ternhill.

The mother was airlifted to hospital with multiple injuries and the sister treated at a separate hospital for serious head and chest injuries.

In Oxford a 22-year-old woman travelling in a people carrier with her two young ...

... the A40 near Brecon when his car was hit by a large branch. He died before an ambulance crew could free him.

An angler swept into the sea at Portlethen, Aberdeenshire, was the seventh victim. He was rescued and taken by RAF helicopter to hospital, but died despite attempts to revive him.

Matthew Ware of the East Anglian Ambulance Service said: "It's been an utterly tragic morning for us. We've had a lot of problems actually getting to the scenes of accidents because of blocked roads."

Others had narrow escapes. Two children were rescued from the sea by police at Salcombe, Devon, while a third was found clinging to a nearby cliff face.

... into the water as she watched the storm from a seafront walkway.

Also at sea, Royal Navy and RAF helicopter crews struggled for seven hours to rescue a Spanish fisherman from a trawler caught in huge seas 170 miles west of the Scilly Isles.

The highest windspeed recorded was 96mph at Swansea in south Wales in what the Meteorological Office described as a severe autumn storm.

The damage was particularly severe in southern England and Wales, with fallen trees and power lines blocking roads and significant damage done to homes, schools and ...

... Heathrow and Gatwick, and another 30 flights due out of Stansted were abandoned.

The Queen Elizabeth II bridge over the Thames at Dartford was closed, as was the Severn Bridge carrying the M48. Railway services were cancelled as fallen trees and damaged power cables forced line closures.

Virgin Trains cancelled all services at one point, and Great North Eastern Railways halted trains between Doncaster and London.

West Anglia Great Northern's Cambridge to London line was also suspended. South West Trains cancelled services ...

- Types of sentences, e.g. simple, compound or complex
- Vocabulary, e.g. modern, emotive, factual, persuasive

Be prepared to share and compare your conclusions with the rest of the class.

PLENARY

Summarise the ways in which each newspaper has written the story for its audience. Focus in detail on **one** of the newspapers. Remember to use your *notes* and give *examples.*

Can you explain, with examples, how papers can present the same event differently?

03 News and Youth

OBJECTIVES *S13a*, S14, TR3, TR10

- To recognise and use stylistic conventions of the main forms of writing used in subjects, e.g. *science report, book review*
- To compare and contrast the ways information is presented in different forms, e.g. *web page, diagrams, prose*
- To identify how media texts are tailored to suit their audience, and recognise that audience responses vary, e.g. *popular websites*

In this section you will look at the ways in which news is packaged for a younger audience.

STARTER

Where do You get your News from?

Complete the grid below with a partner, listing which of the following sources you use to gather news and how useful you find them: Television, Teletext, Internet, Newspapers, Pagers/Mobile phones. Run through the Radio example as a class before you begin.

Form	I use	Partner uses	How Useful?
Radio (e.g. Newsbeat)	Kiss F.M. because I like to listen to music mostly but I will listen to the brief bits of news on the hour.	Capital Radio because I like the chart countdown. The station gives local news in every programme but only broadcasts national news hourly.	It is really annoying to have the D.J chatting over the music and cutting tracks short. Audiences skip to other stations when the ads or news come on. I prefer to watch the news.

INTRODUCTION

Attracting the Target Audience

Look back at the news sources you came up with. All of these try to put their messages across in a way that is attractive to their audience. The page opposite is taken from *The Funday Times*, which is *The Sunday Times*' Junior supplement. This is its News page.

With a partner, make notes on the ways in which *The Funday Times* makes itself attractive to its audience. Consider each of the following style features.

- Typography (the style and appearance of words on the page),
- Layout: columns, size
- Headlines
- Tone (how the language 'sounds': humorous, critical; what opinion it gives)
- Illustration
- Colour

Use this example to guide you:

Typography: the way the word 'news' is illustrated with brightly-coloured icons is more like a magazine or even a comic than a typical newspaper. This would appeal to younger audiences.

Join with another pair and make notes on what kinds of news are being offered (the content).

- For each news item, briefly describe the topic or story being covered.
- Do you find the stories interesting? Why? Try to give word and sentence level examples of text that grabs and keeps your interest.
- How do they compare to the kinds of news you find in 'adult' newspapers? Think about the topic and length.

THE FUNDAY TIMES news

The funny bunnies

Longleat Safari Park, famous for its pride of lions, is now home to another breed with fluffy manes – lionhead rabbits! The rare bunnies originated in Belgium 10 years ago, and have been so popular with park visitors that Longleat bosses have decided to set up a breeding colony. Shortly after lionhead rabbits are born they grow a mass of fur all over their body and then shed it all after a few months, except for the mane. Darren Beasley, the Wiltshire park's rabbit keeper, is more than happy to look after the newcomers. 'Although they are a bit of a dead ringer for a lion, they are a lot less of a handful than the real thing!' he jokes.

Crazy carvings

This sculpture in South Dakota, America, is of the Native American Crazy Horse, the Sioux chief who helped defeat General Custer at the Battle of the Little Big Horn. The Polish sculptor, Korczak Ziolkowski, began work on Crazy Horse in 1948, after Chief Henry Standing Bear of the Sioux tribe asked him to build a monument to their great leader. It's the biggest sculpture in the world although it isn't finished yet! The head alone is nearly 28m high and although it may look like the sculpture's almost complete, there is still the upper body and the head of the chief's horse to come. Korczak died in 1982, and since then his children and grandchildren have been working on the sculpture.

Let's jump around

Britain is set to rock'n'roll as students across the country take part in a national scientific experiment, The Giant Jump, in an attempt to create a new Guinness World Record. The Giant Jump launches Science Year, and will leap into action on Friday, September 7, at 11am. Everyone taking part has to jump up and down for one minute while earthquake detectors monitor the impact it has on the Earth. When rock band Oasis played in London's Earl's Court in 1995, people from up to 1.5km away contacted Scotland Yard claiming they felt a mini-earthquake! There were only 20,000 fans jumping around then, so imagine what millions of students will do. To register your class, go to www.scienceyear.com and prepare to take a giant leap for mankind.

Old bones

When Susan Sibborn found a few bones in her back garden in Humberside, she was relieved to be told that they were too old to warrant a criminal investigation. Fourteen years on, Susan has learnt that she is sitting on an archaeological goldmine that could solve a 1,300-year-old Anglo Saxon mystery. Archaeology experts from Sheffield University found dozens of skeletons and Anglo Saxon artefacts, and believe that Susan's house, in the village of Whitton, is on the site of a monastery built by Etheldreda, the seventh century queen who later became a Catholic saint. It was previously thought to be in the nearby village of West Halton.

Once you have gathered your information on style and content, each group will explain one of these points to the class.

Development

Writing a Story

As a class, decide on three or four stories that you think would be appropriate for *The Funday Times*. Then select one of these stories and think about the **information** the first two paragraphs need to cover.

Write the first paragraph together. Remember to answer the questions: who/what/when/where/why/how? and to grab the reader's attention straight away.

Now, in groups, write the second paragraph. Remember to give more detail, at this point, on one or two of the questions above.

Working on your own, copy out the first two paragraphs and then complete the story, keeping it to 150 words. Finally, think of a catchy headline.

Plenary

Compare the examples of news stories as they are presented and analyse *how* they are different.

Focus on the words and sentences chosen and how each story targets a younger audience.

04 Reviewing Music

OBJECTIVES *S13e*, TR10, TR13, TW15

- **To identify how media texts are tailored to suit their audience, and recognise that audience responses vary, e.g. *popular websites***
- **To identify, using appropriate terminology the way writers of non-fiction texts match language and organisation to their intentions, e.g. *in campaign material***
- **To express a personal view, adding persuasive emphasis to key points, e.g. *by reiteration, exaggeration, repetition, use of rhetorical questions***

In this lesson you get a chance to look at the kind of persuasive writing that appears in reviews in music papers and magazines.

STARTER

How do You get your Music?

Here is a list of different sources of music: Radio, CDs, Live Music, Music TV, Internet, Music Magazines.

Take each source and explain briefly how it is used by people in a table like the one below.

The Radio example has been modelled for you.

Which do you think is the most popular source? You may want to conduct a quick class survey to find out.

Source	How it is used	Preference (out of 10)
Radio	In the car	8 because I can have it quite loud
	In my bedroom	10 because I use my ear phones and have it mega loud
	When I am walking	7 it keeps me company but I feel silly nodding my head in public

INFO

Reviews

The purpose of a magazine or newspaper review is to tell you what's on offer and whether it's any good or not. When you read a review, you will find that it often presents information through a mixture of persuasive writing and discursive writing (designed to present a logical argument).

INTRODUCTION

The Language of Reviews

The language of music reviews is influenced by their subject and by **target audience**, which tends to be young and 'hip'.

Explain what you understand by each word in the list below, taken from music reviews. Can you think of a song or type of music that the word would apply to? The first one has been modelled for you.

- Debut – the first ever single or album released by an artist to launch their careers and to test out the market. If the first release fails, the artist/product will be repackaged.
- Cool
- Catchy
- Buzzy
- Cult

The page opposite consists of a series of single reviews from the magazine *Smash Hits*. Find examples of the following and explain your choices. Language that is:

- 'hip', 'young', 'in-group'
- humorous
- emotive or dramatic

Feed back to the rest of the class.

The lowdown

Smash! Hits SAYS: Sizzling (5 pans) · Hot stuff (4) · Frying tonight (3) · Non stick (2) · Burnt leftovers (1)

APPLETON

Don't Worry

A cheery offering. Not

After going all rawk on us, the terrible twosome are back with a slightly different sound. According to Nat, this dreamy, mellow ballad was written about talking to the dead. OK then, not the most cheery of subjects to sing about, but it's actually a surprisingly sweet and touching track. Nice one girls.

Serena Lacey

TURIN BRAKES

Pain Killer

No pain, all pleasure

You know that feeling of immense joy you have when you get a snog? Or the fluttering you get in your tummy when you find out that someone you've like for ages fancies you? That's euphoria, that is. It's pretty unlikely then that two men with guitars can inspire the same emotion inside you. But, by God, have Turin Brakes done that. This is genius.

Matt Mason

LEANN RIMES

Suddenly

Dad rock

This song was written by someone called Desmond and, according to LeAnn's people, it's got "a powerful rock edge". What are the chances of it not sounding like something your dad would listen to, then? Slimmer than a Cheeky Girl, we'd say. Yep, it sounds like Bon Jovi. Your dad will love it.

Matt Mason

MELANIE C

Here it Comes Again

Return of the Spice

Once you've been as phenomenally successful as a Spice Girl, you need time out, time to chill, time to make some new friends and work on your music. That's just what Mel did and, after a year out of the limelight, she's finally back. Although we might not have realised we missed her while she was away, now that she's back we remember just how good she really is.

Serena Lacey

DEVELOPMENT

Opinions v Facts

Having looked at the language style of music reviews, you are going to focus on the **information** and the **opinions** offered in them. With a partner, choose three of the reviews and write answers to the following questions:

- What have you learnt about the recording and the artiste (Who? What? When?)
- What have you learnt about how 'good' the reviewer thinks it is?
- Which review is best for 'facts' and which for 'opinions'?
- How does the style of the text persuade the reader? (e.g. It may be humorous, cheeky, rebellious.)
- How does the layout appeal to the reader? e.g. Is there a photograph of the artiste(s)?

Taking an album or single of your choice, write a *Smash Hits*-style review of around 70 words.

Try to include these features used by reviewers:

Review checklist

- Exaggerated points about the artiste/product
- Unique selling point
- Present tense
- Short, snappy sentences
- Second person (you)
- Informal language

PLENARY

Present your music review to the class.

Reflect on what have you learnt about music reviews. Write down two suggestions for improving the style of your review.

05 Analysing Soap Opera

OBJECTIVES TR10, TR11, SL6

- **To identify how media texts are tailored to suit their audience, and recognise that audience responses vary, e.g. *popular websites***
- **To recognise how print, sounds and still or moving images combine to create meaning**
- **To listen for and recall the main points of a talk, reading or television programme, reflecting on what has been heard to ask searching questions, make comments or challenge the views expressed**

Extra Resources

Necessary: Introduction – a recording of the start of two popular TV soap operas, including title sequences.

In the lesson you will learn about 'soap opera' and what makes it so popular with viewers.

STARTER

Naming a Soap Opera

To help attract big audiences soaps are given titles that producers hope will appeal to the people likely to watch them.

For each of the soap opera titles below write down what the name suggests and what you think people are likely to associate with it. Follow the example completed for *Coronation Street*.

Coronation Street -It is a 'street' and not an 'avenue' or 'lane' so it suggests it is a place where everyday people live. But, when we consider 'Coronation' it is clear that it refers to royalty and the important historical moment when a princess/prince becomes a Queen/King. So, this street is typically British and is likely to represent a British community.

Eastenders

Hollyoaks

Brookside

Neighbours

Be prepared to give feedback to the class.

INFO

Did They Get The Name Right?

The original name planned for *Coronation Street* when it started back in the early 1960s was *Florizel Street*. This was later changed to *Jubilee Street* until the present title, *Coronation Street* was settled on.

INTRODUCTION

What Makes us Watch Soaps?

Consider the page opposite, taken from a TV listings magazine. It is designed to tell audiences about the coming week's soap episodes by whetting their appetites. This is all part of marketing the 'soap' product.

Below are some of the reasons it has been suggested that people watch soaps. For each reason find an example from the TV listing that would show how this might be the case. Be prepared to feed back your ideas.

- Offering a sense of community
- Docu-drama - very realistic situations
- Identification with characters
- Seeing people in worse situations than your own
- Helping solve your own problems

Discuss whether you think some soaps are better at some of these than others.

DEVELOPMENT

The Opening Sequence

Now look at the title sequences that your teacher will play for you on video. Then copy out the grid shown opposite to help you compare and contrast the two soaps. For each item, explain:

- What it tells the audience about the genre of soap
- How it will appeal to this audience?

Be ready to share your comments with the rest of the class.

Soapzone

CORONATION STREET

Grief has gripped the Street, and Maxine's funeral this week brings not only tears, but accusations and yet another blow for Ashley.

Murderer Richard is losing the plot. When David brings up the subject of Maxine's battered skull, he escapes to the garden wondering whether he'll make it through the funeral without cracking up.

As a silent crowd gathers on the morning of the funeral, Norris wonders aloud whether Richard would have attended if it had been Emily's funeral. This sets Audrey thinking and things suddenly become clear — what if Maxine got in the way of an attempt on Emily's life? She concludes that Richard did indeed kill Maxine.

In the church, Maxine's dad can't bring himself to make a speech and, in an ironic twist, Gail pushes Richard forward to take his place, where he almost confesses to her murder. But to the mourners his genuine remorse looks like grief for a life cut short.

However, Audrey's not willing to let sleeping dogs lie and launches an attack on Richard, publicly accusing him of Maxine's murder...

Meanwhile, Ashley's grief turns to anger when Fred takes a call from his former neighbour and the possible father of baby Josh, Dr Matt Ramsden. He tells him never to call again and confides in Fred that Josh may not be his biological grandson, telling Fred about Maxine and Matt's fling. It slowly dawns on Ashley that Matt may now fight for custody of Josh.

Will Ashley lose his son as well as his wife?

Also in Coronation Street

● Ken persuades Ade's dad to visit his son, but Ade rejects their help. ● Shelley and Sunita make up before Shelley goes to Mexico with Peter. ● Kevin becomes suspicious when Rosie tells him about Craig Nelson writing another name on his school book.

Coronation Street, ITV1 Sun Mon (2 episodes) Wed & Fri

Richard makes a speech

Ashley is devastated at Maxine's funeral

Ashley's double heartache

Dave (right) isn't scared by Pete's

FAMILY AFFAIRS

Conventional features of sequence	Soap 1	Soap 2
Music e.g. pop, classical...		
Setting e.g. street, square		
Title graphics, e.g. font, colour, animation		
Characters introduced (if any), e.g. male/ female/ age/race		

PLENARY

Consider the title sequences you have watched and the reasons you identified for watching soaps. Compose a statement that **summarises** why your class likes watching soaps and also gives reasons for not watching them. Use the model below.

One of the main reasons for watching soap operas is ___________. In addition, an audience aged 11 to 12 years of age may also watch soap operas because ____.

On the other hand, there are convincing reasons not to watch them, for example ____ __________.

To conclude, we think that _____________.

06 Writing Soap Operas

OBJECTIVES TR10, TW5, SL16

- To identify how media texts are tailored to suit their audience, and recognise that audience responses vary, e.g. *popular websites*
- To structure a story with an arresting opening, a developing plot, a complication, a crisis and a satisfying resolution
- To work collaboratively to devise and present scripted and unscripted pieces, which maintain the attention of an audience

Extra Resources

Optional: Development - equipment for filming/photographing storyboard scenes written by pupils, if time allows.

In this lesson you will look at some of the types of character that you are likely to meet in a soap opera and that are often stereotypes of gender, race or class.

STARTER

Character Types

Soap operas rely heavily on certain character types (**stock characters**) in order to represent the range of people in a community and to run the stories as episodes or **multiple narratives**.

Give an example one of each of these character types in a grid like the one below: Nosey Parker, Rebellious teenager, Single parent, Authority figure, Local villain. Draw on characters from soaps that you watch.

Also note what sort of storyline the character is most likely to feature in. The 'Grumpy pensioner' character has been modelled for you.

Stereotype	Grumpy pensioner
Character	Dot
Programme	EastEnders
Storyline	Dot has recently re-married and is very religious. She is the local gossip but also the 'nagging wife. She is often involved in the lightweight stories such as hatching budgie eggs in her cupboard.

Be prepared to share your ideas with the rest of the class.

INTRODUCTION

School Life as a Soap

Imagine a new soap opera is to be based on life in your school

Working groups of four, first decide which one of the storylines in the grid on page 19 to develop as your pilot episode.

Now brainstorm some ideas to help get the programme running. You will need your notes later to plan the first scene. Try to decide:

- Who would be the main characters? You need villains as well as heroes.
- Which places in and around the school would make good locations for scenes in the soap?

DEVELOPMENT

Scripting your First Scene

Now you are going to develop a scripted establishing scene for the first episode of your soap opera.

Review your brainstorm notes and your chosen storyline. Remember that as this is the **pilot episode**, the audience will need to get know your characters; they will not yet be familiar with them.

Think carefully about the following conventions of a TV script.

Directions for:
- The setting/location
- Time
- Weather
- What the characters are doing, e.g. walking in the street
- Appearance, e.g. age/hair/clothes

Details of:
- Camera angles/shots
- Cuts
- Fades

Plot	Story 1	Story 2
Establishing scene	Year 7 First week at school Student X is nervous	Student x is very quiet Has one close friend Works quite hard in lessons
Complication	Some kids bullying X Tutor too busy X begins to truant some lessons X very moody/ aggressive at home	Writes an essay in English about Chat rooms Teacher sees x at break X lies- says it was fantasy
Further complication	Fight at home Becomes unwell (depression/ eating disorder) In trouble at school; no homework/bad attitude	Teacher shows it to deputy head Decide to do nothing/ stay alert X spends every evening in chat room Arranges date with stranger in another town
Crisis	X and other truanters ride the buses/tube They steal/don't pay fares Caught by police Returned to school Parents contacted	X tells close friend Friend advises NOT to go X takes coach to next town, far away Meets older date in car park, alone Parents v worried X not home
Resolution	Bully and bullied attend school counselling X still truants Tutor pays more attention Parents still very worried	Teacher confronts X. X tells truth T and X meet parents Date still posts abusive messages in chat room. X now very scared...

INFO

Pilot Episodes

Before a TV company will spend money on a new programme like a soap opera, they produce a 'pilot' to experiment with. The pilot is first trialled on the 'target audience'. If the audience response is poor, then the programme is not pursued. If the response is good, a series is commissioned.

(For more on the types of shot you might include, read pages 116-119.)

Use the example script opposite to follow these conventions in your own draft. Your scene should last 1 minute 30 seconds.

PLENARY

Watch as each scene is read or performed to the class.

As you watch other groups, assess how successfully the list of TV script conventions is used. Offer ideas for how the episode might be improved.

SCENE 1

[running time 1 minute 30 seconds]

FADE UP FROM TITLE SEQUENCE TO:

Ext. Road outside the school gates. 8.30am The weather is overcast

Ryan is getting out of his father's car. Dan and Tom are standing by the gate kicking stones into the gutter.

Ryan: (shutting the car door) Yeah sure Dad. I'll be okay. You don't need to come with me.

Dan: (to Tom) I've never seen him before. D'you think he's new?

Tom: Poor kid. He won't know what's hit him.

CUT TO...

07 Popular Game Shows

OBJECTIVES TR10, SL6, SL8, SL16

- **To identify how media texts are tailored to suit their audience, and recognise that audience responses vary, e.g. *popular websites***
- **To listen for and recall the main points of a talk, reading or television programme, reflecting on what has been heard to ask searching questions, make comments or challenge the views expressed**
- **To identify the main methods used by presenters to explain, persuade, amuse or argue a case, e.g. *emotive vocabulary, verbal humour***
- **To work collaboratively to devise and present scripted and unscripted pieces, which maintain the attention of an audience**

In this lesson you will consider what makes the game show Blind Date so appealing and popular.

Extra Resources

Optional: Introduction - a recording of *Blind Date.*

INFO

BLIND DATE PROFILE

Blind Date's Saturday night audiences peak at around 8 million or 37% of all viewers watching TV at the time. The show appeals particularly to 16-34 year olds. In its eighteenth year, *Blind Date* reached 60% of all viewing individuals at some time.

STARTER

Language of the Script

Like most game shows, the contestants and audience of *Blind Date* are chosen from members of the public. The ages of the contestants vary but the basic formula relies on a man choosing from three women or a woman choosing from three men.

Read the text from a *Blind Date* script on page 21, concentrating on what is said by the presenter, Cilla Black, and by the contestants. Think about the words and sentences which keep the audience's interest and entertain them. Note down examples of:

- Puns
- Rhyme
- Gender stereotypical language, e.g. sexy/macho...
- Open questions, e.g. don't you think...?
- Informal language- slang
- Rhetorical questions
- Direct address to audience

Be prepared to share your findings with the rest of the class.

INTRODUCTION

Looking at the 'Ingredients'

Now, using the still showing the set on page 21 and the text from the script, consider some of the other ingredients of *Blind Date*. For each one, make notes describing the part it plays in the show and its success.

- The set
- The music
- The appearance/voice of contestants
- The presenter
- Audience laughter/response

Note: if you do have access to a clip from *Blind Date* this would aid your analysis.

Be ready to share your conclusions with the rest of the class.

Cilla: But first, let's meet 3 lads hoping to be leaving *Blind Date* with love tonight. Here they are:

Contestant 1: Hi, my name's Alex, I'm 25 and I'm a designer from Surrey. (Audience cheers)

The reason I'm on *Blind Date* tonight is because I'm looking for a girl that's not going to get completely crazy about me. (Audience laughs) All my ex's have been obsessive, possessive and aggressive, so I'm looking for a more laid back type

(Audience laughs)

Cilla: Whoa!...

[Contestants 2 and 3 introduce themselves. One is Lawrence, an electrical retailer from Northhampton who likes women to wear stilettos, and Liam, a butcher from Rochdale]

Cilla: Well, there you have it. Three of them all looking for love, but only one will walk away with our gorgeous girl tonight. And who's the lucky lady? She's luscious, she's Lucy and she's from Hertfordshire. Come in, Lucy.

(Audience cheers)

Cilla: I have to say you look stunning, girl, and what a pair of stilettos! Tell everybody what you do.

Lucy: I'm a broadcast journalism student from Nottingham Trent University, Cilla.

Cilla: Wonderful, now you're determined to find the right man for you here on *Blind Date* tonight.

Lucy: I am, Cilla...

Cilla: Fire away with your first question.

Lucy: Hello boys!

(Audience laughs)

Contestants: Hello, Lucy!

Lucy: Okay this is question one. I've recently had my palm read and I was told that I have an independent streak and I'm very strong-willed. How would you handle this if we got into an argument?...

Contestant 1: Well, Lucy, I too have had my palms read recently and I've been told that I was independent, funny and great boyfriend material. So instead of worrying about how we'd handle an argument, let's work on how we're going to kiss and make up.

Lucy: Oooh!

DEVELOPMENT

Questions and Answers

You are going to write a *Blind Date* simulation. Your role will be either as a 'Picker', a 'Contestant' or a 'Presenter'.

- The Picker will write down three questions that might be used on *Blind Date*. Remember the show has a family audience so you will need to ask suitable questions.
- The three Contestants will work out what type of personality to portray, e.g. sporty, cheeky. And then they will script their own answers to the Picker's questions using language to persuade her/him to choose them.
- The Presenter will script the linking lines between the Picker and the Contestants.

Remember to use the language features listed on page 20 in your script to maintain the audience's interest and to entertain them.

PLENARY

Each group should act out their simulation for the class. For each group, think about how persuasive and entertaining the language is. Bear these three questions in mind:

- How effective the questions are from contestants
- How successfully the personalities come across
- How successful contestants' answers are

08 Interactive TV

OBJECTIVES TR3, TR11, TW10

- To compare and contrast the ways information is presented in different forms, e.g. *web page, diagrams, prose*
- To recognise how print, sounds and still or moving images combine to create meaning
- To organise texts in ways appropriate to their context, e.g. *by chronology, priority, comparison,* and signpost this clearly to the reader

Extra Resources

Optional: Development - recorded TV programmes that could be made interactive.

In this lesson you will look at information writing for interactive digital television.

STARTER

Texts on Screen

Here are some of the ways in which text or worded graphics appear on our television screens: Caption Subtitle Title Credit Teletext Interactive menu

Copy the table below and give an explanation for each term. Then make brief notes on the purpose of each, following the example given for Caption.

TV Text	Explanation	Purpose
Caption	This is a short written sentence placed below or near to an image.	It is used to inform the reader about the image content by offering more detail. It helps us 'read' the image in a particular way.

INTRODUCTION

What Makes It Interactive?

The large image on page 23 is a main menu frame from the BBC series *Walking with Beasts*, which focuses on pre-historic insect-hunters. The television screen partly resembles a computer screen with frames of information that the viewer can 'interact' with.

PC

Make notes to show how computer-style images and text are being used to complement the information already offered by the non-interactive version. Consider three areas, following the model opposite:

- Presentational devices - the appearance/'look' of the screen
- Content - the types of information available to the viewer
- The style - the use of particular words and phrases

Content - the viewer is offered an 'In-depth narration' which gives more detail about the creatures than the original programme has time for.

The three smaller images opposite are the sub-menu frames that can be called up from the main menu. Examine the way in which each frame uses:

- caption text to deliver specific information
- inset images

INFO

Digital Broadcasting

The advent of this medium (where programmes are delivered by cable or by satellite) has allowed television to become interactive. A viewer whose set is connected to a phone line can use their remote control to choose and in some cases what is on the screen. This can include everything from voting in a viewers' poll to ordering a pizza.

DEVELOPMENT

Interactive Viewing

Use the *Walking with Beasts* example frames to help you devise your own main menu and sub-menus for a part of a programme of your choosing. It may help to view a clip from the show you are going to use.

- Start by deciding on the main frame content.
- Think about what the viewers would like to know more about. Use these topics as the titles of your sub-menus
- Write a sub-menu for one of your titles – using caption-style text and suggesting an image to go with it.

Main frame content: commentators talking before a premiership football match begins.

Sub-menu titles: Manchester United - Games ahead this season; Player feature; Formations to be used

Sub-menu - Player feature: Rio Ferdinand - Ferdinand scored his first goal in the Premiership for West Ham against Sheffield Utd in 1996.

PLENARY

Present your main menu, sub-menu and interactive text to the class. Consider how well:

- The main menu targets the audience for the programme type through the sub-menu titles
- Key information is conveyed in the sub-menu text

Using your new understanding discuss the following:

- What would you say Interactive TV adds to your viewing?
- What do you still need to find out Interactive TV?

09 Pop Promotion

OBJECTIVES *TR4*, TR8, TW10, SL12

- **To identify how meanings are implied by the words and texts**
- **To organise texts in ways appropriate to their content e.g. *by chronology, priority, comparison*, and signpost this clearly to the reader**
- **To use exploratory, hypothetical and speculative talk as a way of researching ideas and expanding thinking**

Extra Resources

Optional: Introduction and Development – pictures of current pop-bands

In this lesson you will explore the importance of pop groups' names and images in appealing to their audience, and how different media are used to promote them.

STARTER

What's in a Name?

The name that a band or artiste chooses is an important element in gaining recognition from the public. A band's name will create associations and a unique 'image' in their audiences' minds: the first step in **branding**.

Below are the names of pop stars and groups from different eras. For each one, note down:

- The kind of ideas they are trying to promote, e.g. about being young, male/female
- The image they are trying to create, e.g. sexy, hard, wild
- The genre of music they might produce, e.g. rock and roll, classical, pop.

Use the example below to guide you. Be prepared to share your ideas with the class.

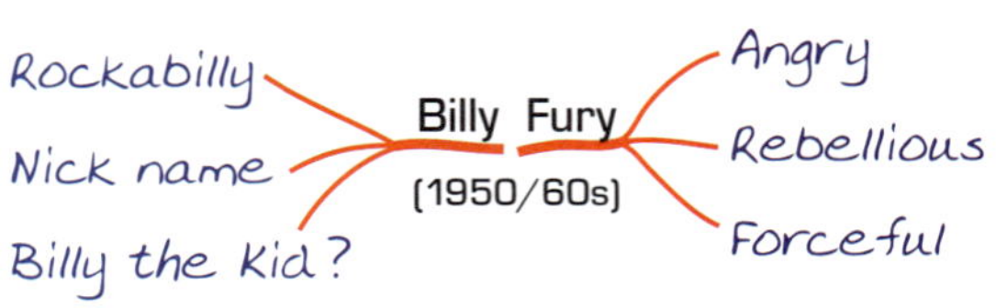

INFO

Unique Selling Point (USP)

Most products sell better if they offer something to their target audience that no other product can – something unique. Whether the product is shampoo or a pop band, them are trying to offer a unique selling point or USP to their audience.

INTRODUCTION

Name, Image and Identity

Now look at the pictures opposite. Can you match the right names to the pictures? Discuss any differences of interpretation you may have. Explain your opinion clearly and relate it to the image/name.

- Adam Ant (1980s)
- The Sex Pistols (1970s)
- The Grateful Dead (1960/70s)
- The Cure (1980/90s)
- All Saints (1990s)
- Public Enemy (1980/90s)
- Snoop Dogg (1990s/2000s)

Imagine that you have been asked to make suggestions for forming a new band that appeals to your age group. Talk through all the questions, making notes on each.

- What is the unique selling point of your band?
- What name will you give your band and why?
- How many members will it have and how many will be female/male?
- Will they all play instruments? Which ones?
- How will they look? Think about hair, dress and make-up.

Be prepared to present your ideas to the rest of the class.

DEVELOPMENT

Promoting your Band

Record companies use a variety of ways to bring a band to the public's attention, for example posters, radio and television interviews. The first step is usually a **press release.**

In your groups write a press release for your new band announcing its first national tour. Use the writing frame below to guide you.

Press Release

Opening para Informs the reader what the press release is about, e.g. name of star, type of music, the fact they are about to tour

Para 2 Offers details of the tour e.g. dates, venues, guests/support bands

Para 3 Reminds why the star is so different/ special: unusual voice/writes own lyrics/ plays instruments – why this will be a special tour

Before you write your review read the list of press release features on page 29.

PLENARY

Listen as groups read out their press releases. Make notes on the following questions:

- Does the text promote the image of the new band?
- Is all the important information about the tour included?
- Is the order of the information logical and helpful?

10 Making Popstars

OBJECTIVES TR10, TR11, TR13, TW10

- To identify how media texts are tailored to suit their audience, and recognise that audience responses vary, e.g. *popular websites*
- To recognise how print, sounds and still or moving images combine to create meaning
- To identify, using appropriate terminology the way writers of non-fiction match language and organisation to their intentions, e.g. *in campaign material*
- To organise texts in ways appropriate to their context, e.g. *by chronology, priority, comparison,* and signpost this clearly to the reader

Extra Resources

Necessary: Introduction and Development – clip from a recent pop idol type band video.

In this lesson you will think about the way media products are designed to appeal to their audience by looking at the creation of a pop group.

STARTER

The Spice Girls – Real or 'Man-made'?

The group the Spice Girls pictured on page 27 caused a sensation when they were formed in 1994 They were 'packaged' to appeal to a wide market of young women and men. Part of their 'Unique Selling Point' was to give each member of the band a separate image and personality whilst also being part of the Spice gang:

- Sporty's was athletic and serious
- Baby was the innocent blonde
- Scary was outspoken and feisty
- Posh was the quiet, elegant one
- Ginger was the flamboyant one

Look carefully at the two images on page 27. Then make notes on a copy of the grid below to identify the ways in which the group is meant to appeal to their audience. For each entry in the grid **describe** how it appears in the photograph and then try to **explain** what it tells us about the band's image.

Spice Girls	Description from photos	Differences between 2 phases
A mix of:		
Age		
Gender		
Race		
Individual members:		
Hair		
Clothing/colours		
Personality		
Style		
Dance		

INTRODUCTION

Image and Sound

Now watch a video clip of a pop band *without the sound*. As you do so, use a note frame like this to help you answer the questions below.

Feature	Your views
Story: what happens	
Setting: e.g. street/bedroom/lake	
Special effects	
How does the video end? Are there any unanswered questions?	
Who is the main 'character' and why?	

Watch the video clip again with the sound and then complete the notes below.

Feature	Your views
Sound: e.g. song/ silence/voice-over/ special effects?	
Other details	

INFO

The Band As A Product

The Spice Girls were one of the first highly-manufactured bands. The TV series *Pop Stars* made the auditioning process of bands a form of popular TV entertainment. Programmes such as *Pop Idol* took this further, allowing audiences to interact through telephone voting, and to choose who should go on to stardom.

Ginger Spice gets a new role as UN ambassador

BY JESSICA CALLAN

THE former Spice Girl Geri Halliwell will follow in the film star footsteps of Audrey Hepburn and Roger Moore by becoming a goodwill ambassador for the United Nations.
The 26-year-old pop singer flew to New York yesterday to be appointed as Britain's ambassador for the UN population fund. The former Ginger Spice will also work with the Marie Stopes charity, the worldwide family planning organisation.
Halliwell, who left the group in May, is reported to have signed a £2 million solo record deal with Chrysalis Records. Last week, she was filming a report in Uganda for Comic Relief and she recently promoted breast cancer awareness.
She has visited inmates at Holloway Prison, and a London school to highlight the dangers of the disease after she had a breast cancer scare when she was 18.
She auctioned her Spice Girls stage costumes last month, which raised £150,000 for Sargent, a children's cancer charity.

Geri Halliwell: Goodwill Ambassador

THE DAILY TELEGRAPH Tuesday, October 20, 1998

DEVELOPMENT

Repackaging Gerri

When Gerri Haliwell, Ginger Spice, decided to leave the Spice Girls in 1998, her aim was a solo career, but also to work in other areas, such as international relations.

Using the information in the newspaper extract and the writing frame on page 29, write a press release to relaunch Gerri's career.

Try to use a maximum of 200 words and refer to the list of press release features on page 29.

<u>Press Release - Gerri's latest news</u>

<u>Para 1</u> Gives latest on Gerri Hallliwell - her trip to New York and new UN role

<u>Para 2</u> Gerri's immediate plans - launch solo career, new record deal details

<u>Para 3</u> Gerri's longer term plans - exact nature of UN role/cancer fundraising and awareness

<u>Para 4</u> Reminder of Gerri's main strengths as a performer/ celebrity - sale of Spice Girls costumes for charity

End on up-beat note about her future career

Include as many of these features as you can in your press release.

<u>Press release features</u>

<u>Present tense</u>, to give a sense of immediacy , e.g. Craig David comes to Leeds this week or future tense, e.g. Missy Elliot will rock the house at Brixton on Friday

<u>Persuasive language</u>, to imply this band is the best e.g. no one can beat Missy Elliot and her crew when the rap begins

<u>Rhetorical devices</u>, open questions, encouraging use of imperative, e.g. Would you really want to miss this one? Come on - it's not everyday that Oasis....

<u>Alliteration</u>, repeated letters to make phrases memorable, e.g. Gorgeous Gareth has girls getting giggy-with-it in Gloucester

<u>Style</u>: informal/ chatty, using 'cool' vocabulary

PLENARY

Listen as pairs read out different paragraphs of their press releases.

Then offer feedback on how successful they were in getting key information across concisely and in an appealing way. Refer to the list of press release features above to help you.

11 Love Lyrics

OBJECTIVES TR7, TR8, TR11, TR14

- **To identify the main points, processes or ideas in a text and how they are sequenced and developed by the writer;**
- **To infer and deduce meanings using evidence in the text, identifying where and how meanings are implied;**
- **To recognise how print, sounds and still or moving images combine to create meaning**
- **To recognise how writers' language choices can enhance meaning, e.g. *repetition, emotive vocabulary, varied sentence structure or line length, sound effects***

In this lesson you will look at the words, or lyrics, of popular songs.

STARTER

Typical Love Lyrics

With your partner brainstorm the titles of some popular love songs you have heard. Now write down five words or ideas about love that you think appear most often in the love songs and say why you think these words are so popular. Here is one to get you started.

Babe/baby - these are terms used for the young woman or man who is the subject of the song. They suggest that she/he is young and needs protecting like a baby and that the singer is the only one who can do this.

INTRODUCTION

A Closer Look at Lyrics

PC

Read the Ms Dynamite lyrics on page 31 carefully. Then annotate the lyrics finding evidence to support your answers to the following.

- How is rhyme used in the lyrics to create an effect, e.g. to make it 'catchy' and easy to remember? Does it use rhyming couplets?
- How does the song use non-standard English?
- Why does the song include some conventions of text messaging?
- What effect does the use of assonance and other forms of repetition have?
- What is the role of the chorus?
- What is the overall appeal of the song to listeners?

DEVELOPMENT

The Story in a Song

Your may have noticed when analysing the song's language that *Dy-na-mi-tee* tells the story of the singer's childhood and teenage years.

Look again at the lyrics and try to plot out the story they tell verse by verse. Use a grid like the one below to help you summarise the narrative.

	Summary of the story told in Dy-na-mi-tee
Verse 1	*Ms Dynamite thinks about how she rebelled as a teenager*
Chorus	
Verse 2	
Verse 3	

PLENARY

Swap your summary with another group. Read theirs carefully and comment to the class on:

- How their interpretations might be improved
- What you thought was successful about their summary.

DY-NA-MI-TEE

Verse 1
Yo I'm that same little girl that grew up next door 2 u
Went through all the things a teenage girl goes through
Hangin' out all night and breaking my curfew
When my daddy hit the door I gave mamma the blues
Use 2 spend my time blazin' lazin' days away
Thought I was grown left home at 15 didn't wanna obey
Had 2 get my act together could'nt take the heat
And now I'm makin' beats for the streets

Chorus
I'm Ms Dy-na-mi-tee
I stay blowin' up ur stereo
I'm just Ms Dy-na-mi-tee
Everybody gotta hear me u
Hear me bussin on da radio
Now feel my flow u get me though
I'm Ms Dy-na-mi-tee
C me bouncin' in da video
And I come 2 rock da show
I'm Ms Dy-na-mi-tee
Everybody loose control
Let my vibe 2uch ur soul

Verse 2
I remember all the house parties that took place
Bein' in my bed upstairs and we could still feel the base
And my cousins and my brothers we'd sit up all night
Listenin' 2 my family vibin' till the mornin' light
Remember my first years of school I was so innocent
I just wanted 2 learn I never been so content
But the more that I learned I found a guidin' light
That showed me the need to fight
And be

Chorus

Verse 3
At 13 I thought that I was in love with this guy
Anytime that I caught his eye I thought that I'd just die
Remember playin' class clown I was just a disruptive fool
And the beatin' that I got first time suspended from school
Remember Sunday school and after go 2 Granmas 4 lunch
Macaroni, rice and peas, chicken and pineapple punch
Never had much my mum brother sister and me
But love was enough 2 succeed
2 grow

Chorus

12 Writing Song Lyrics

OBJECTIVES TR6, TR11, TW8

- **To adopt active reading approaches to engage with and make sense of texts, e.g. *visualising, predicting, empathising and relating to own experience***
- **To recognise how print, sounds and still or moving images combine to create meaning**
- **To experiment with the visual and sound effects of language, including the use of imagery, alliteration, rhythm and rhyme**

Extra Resources

Optional: Development - song lyrics, possibly from a CD inlay card, eg. use Miss Dyanmite song, *Dy-na-mi-tee.*

In this lesson you will have a chance to write your own lyrics for a love song.

STARTER

Using Rhyme

Read these lyrics from different love songs. Consider how each phrase is written and try to explain the effect of each one. What feelings does each evoke? Follow the first example.

OHT

- Who's going to drive you home – a rhetorical question – is the singer his girl or jealous?
- Strangers in the night exchanging glances
- One love, for the mother's pride, One love for the days you've cried
- My love is like the wind

Song lyrics usually rely on rhyme to achieve an effect. Here are some words that are often heard in love songs. For each one suggest two words that would make an appropriate rhyme. The first one has been done for you.

- Boy e.g. toy, joy
- Girl
- Love
- Heart
- Chance
- Eyes
- Smile

INTRODUCTION

Catchy Choruses

Songs usually have a chorus: two to four lines that rhyme and are repeated between verses in the song. Choruses are often the parts of songs that most people remember.

Write a four-line chorus to follow the first verse of the song below about falling out of love. You will need to decide if the singer is rejecting the boy/girlfriend or if they are being rejected.

Make the chorus memorable and catchy.

- Use rhyme: be/see
- Use imagery, e.g. similes: you are like bad news on CNN
- Play with the language: I should go back 2 skool/I wanna
- Keep the lines short
- Abbreviate some words: hangin' lazin'
- Use the first person: 'I'

Verse 1

It couldn't be, they said it could never be

We talked through it all and then I could see

As my heart woke to all that you are

It couldn't be, they said that you were by far

The best

DEVELOPMENT

Writing Your Lyrics

Work together to map out the rest of the story for your song. Then write two more verses.

- Use Verse 2 to present happy memories about the relationship (see example lyrics for Verse 2 on page 33).
- Use Verse 3 to look ahead to what lies beyond this break up.

- Make any changes that may be necessary to your original chorus.

> ***Verse 2***
>
> *It couldn't be, they said it could never be*
>
> *But I think about the good times and then I see …*

Decide together what kind of music would best suit your completed lyrics. Who would you like to sing them? Be prepared to share your reasons with the rest of the class.

PLENARY

Consider some of the song lyrics that have been written.

Choose two and come up with ideas for how you would promote them to ensure they are hits.

- On what TV or radio channel would the song first be heard?
- Who would interview your artiste/band first?

13 Reading Between Lines and Beyond Images

OBJECTIVES *TR4*, TR8, TR10, TR11

- **To infer and deduce meanings using evidence in the text, identifying where and how meanings are implied**
- **To identify how media texts are tailored to suit their audience, and recognise that audience responses vary, e.g. *popular websites***
- **To recognise how print, sounds and still or moving images combine to create meaning**

Extra Resources

Necessary: Starter – five copies of glossy magazines for advertisement editorial analysis.

In this lesson you will look at the ways in which we advertisements in magazines can be 'read'.

STARTER

Magazine Target Groups

In groups, look through the copy of a glossy magazine you have been given. Consider carefully the target audience for the magazine. Read the **editorial** to help you do this. Now fill in the grid below together.

	Magazine Audience Evidence: images/ language used
Gender	
Age	
Social class/ ethnicity	
Educational background	

Share your findings with the rest of the class.

INFO

Advertising As Funding

Magazines are funded by a combination of their cover price and money from advertising. The advertisement on pg 35 comes from a magazine which is 40% advertisements and has a circulation figure of 330,000. A full-page advertisement in a prime position in the magazine costs up to £14,000.

INTRODUCTION

What's in an Ad?

Glossy magazine advertisements are often sophisticated texts even if their central messages are fairly simple.

Remember that advertisements are designed to **persuade** readers to buy a product. Part of this technique is to make a person think that they need a product whether they need it or not.

Now take a close look at the advertisement on pg 35 and answer these questions. Be prepared to feedback to the class.

- What are your first impressions?
- Who is trying to communicate with you?
- What does it consist of, e.g. image, logo, print?
- What are the most important parts of it, e.g. shoutline, illustration, background, etc.?
- What is the style of presentation, e.g. colourful, striking, 'busy'?
- What is the simple message?
- What else is it trying to offer to you, e.g. humour, glamour, a puzzle, etc?

DEVELOPMENT

How Ads Work

It is easy to take things for granted when you first glance at an advertisement. So reconsider the ad on page 35 by making notes on these questions.

- How is the person presented, e.g. gender, clothes, actions?
- What other objects are presented?
- How many kinds of written text are there?
- What do the words say about the product?

Write a brief **commentary** explaining how the ad suggests qualities about the product to the reader. Draw on the notes you have made so far. The following start of a model answer should also guide you.

The reader's view is directed to the centre top of the page by the positioning and lighting of the model. Her general 'look' suggests assertive qualities. The lighting throws the left-hand side into darkness, placing the emphasis on the model's 'even' makeup – the product itself. The model's crown tatoo in the foreground signifies strength and quality. The shoutline GET EVEN ...

PLENARY

Listen as some commentaries on the advertisement are read out. Make notes on how clearly the writers express their points. Are these points supported by evidence and evaluation?

Offer your feedback in class discussion.

14 The Language of Advertising

OBJECTIVES *S13e*, TR10, TR11, *TW1*, TW8

- **To identify how media texts are created to suit their audience**
- **To recognise how print, sounds and still or moving images combine to create meaning**
- **To experiment with the visual and sound effects of language, including the use of imagery, alliteration, rhythm and rhyme**

Extra Resources

Optional: Development – other car advertisements from glossy magazines or newspaper supplements.

In this lesson you will be considering the skills of the copywriter, the person who writes the words or copy to support the host of visual images that advertising uses.

STARTER

The Importance of Being 'NEW'

Research has shown that the word most used word in advertising copy is 'new'. Why do you think this might be? With a partner, suggest which other words feature heavily in advertisements either on television, in magazines or in newspapers. Map out your ideas in a word web like the one below. You may need a dictionary or thesaurus.

Share your ideas with the class. Which is the most popular word?

Now work with your partner to explain the impression you get from each of these memorable car **slogans**. Use A3 paper to map out your ideas in a spider diagram.

You see more in a Range Rover

Once driven, forever smitten (VAUXHALL)

The lion goes from strength to strength (PEUGEOT)

HONDA: The Power of Dreams

INTRODUCTION

Looking at the Text

Read the Honda advertisement on page 37 paying particular attention to the text or **copy**.

Then answer the questions below and be prepared to feed back to the class.

The text

- What kind of car is the ad persuading readers that the Honda will replace?
- Is the main shoutline 'Bye bye, GTI' memorable? If so why?
- In what other type of writing might you see language such as 'we regret to announce the sad demise...'? Why do you think they are imitating this style?

The whole ad

- What other information are you given about the car? How?
- What arguments are used to try to persuade people?
- What kind of people do you think would be likely to buy this car? From which age group?

DEVELOPMENT

Writing Advertising Copy

Using either the image opposite or one you have chosen, provide new copy for a campaign to sell the car as **one** of the following:

- A family car, i.e. big but cosy, safe, spacious, economical
- Attractive to independent young women, i.e. says what you want it to say, fast, sleek, safe
- Attractive to independent young men, i.e. lean, economical and stylish

You need to be able to explain your choice of language. What tone will you adopt? Will the copy be funny or serious, for example?

Remember to use:

- Adjectives, e.g. safe/ lean
- Expanded noun phrases, e.g. cosy car with more space than yer or'nairy People Carrier!
- Alliteration, e.g. sleek/ slender/packs a punch
- Onomatopoeia, e.g. Va va voom
- Wordplay

Share ideas for a slogan or **catchphrase** for your ad. Choose the most memorable.

Revise the copy until you are ready to **pitch** it to the class. Remember that you do not have many words to play with – most car ads contain between 50 and 70 words.

PLENARY

Listen as groups present the Honda ad for a new audience.

Identify the persuasive language features used in their copy. Give feedback on one aspect that might be improved.

Take a class vote on which is the most persuasive copy.

15 Gender Representation in Advertising

OBJECTIVES TR10, TR11, *TW1*, TW11

- **To identify how media texts are tailored to suit their audience, and recognise that audience responses vary, e.g. *popular websites***
- **To recognise how print, sounds and still or moving images combine to create meaning**
- **To select and present information using detail, example, diagram and illustration as appropriate**

Extra Resources

Optional: Development – other magazine/TV ads depicting interesting gender representations of men and women.

In this lesson you will explore how men and women are represented differently in advertising in newspapers and magazines.

INFO

Connotations

Why do we associate 'sporty' for example, with young men or women who exercise and have a healthy lifestyle? It is because each time that we 'read' a film or an ad we bring our own cultural ideas and feelings to this new text and these help us make sense of it. These are called connotations – the secondary or extra meanings that a word or image carries.

STARTER

Connotations of Words

Here are some words that are used in magazine advertisements aimed at men or women. Explain briefly the **connotations** of each word. Try to decide which gender you think each word is most likely to be aimed at. Explain your reasoning. Use the model below for 'Sporty' to help you.

- Sensual
- Sporty
- Low maintenance
- Non iron
- Crease resistant
- Rugged
- Fragrant

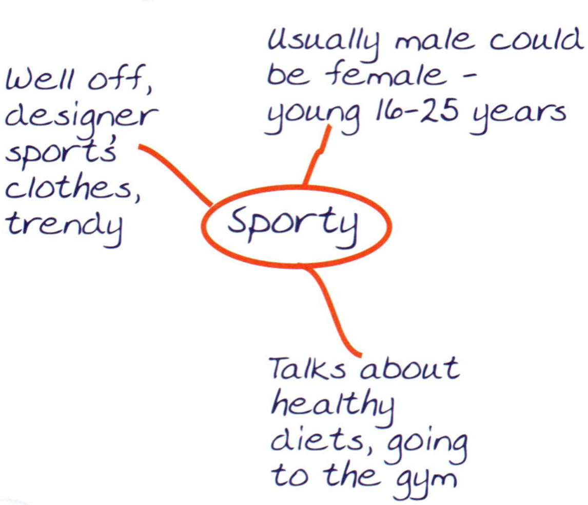

INTRODUCTION

Images of Women and Men

Decide which two groups will cover which of the three advertisements on pages 39-41. Read your chosen advertisement, focusing particularly on how a man and/or a woman are represented in the image. You need to describe in note form:

- The background and foreground
- What they are doing
- Their appearance and their clothes
- How they are posed next to each other
- The angle of the shot
- What they might have been doing before the photograph was taken
- What they might do afterwards
- What product they are being used to sell

Use the model below. Your notes will be needed later when you examine the effect of each ad.

background: The ad is set outdoors in bright sunlight. We can see this from the light reflecting off the second model's clothes and hair. The lighting emphasises the outline of the main model and the phone in her back pocket.

Summarise your findings on your chosen ad for the class.

Then take notes on the other groups' comments on the remaining two ads.

DEVELOPMENT

Implications

Review your notes on the images in the ads on pages 39-41.

Re-evaluate the observations you have made. Explain why each element is included in the ad and its effect in persuading the reader to buy the product.

Now examine the text that accompanies these images. How do they reflect the messages about men and women conveyed by the images?

Review what you have learned about the different ways in which men and women are depicted in advertisements.

Summarise your group's findings like this:

The ads aimed at women use these 3 main techniques to persuade the reader:

Firstly,...

Secondly...

Thirdly...

The ads aimed at men use these 3 main techniques to persuade the reader:

Firstly,...

PLENARY

Feed back your group findings on the ways in which men and women are presented. Make a class poster to summarise these.

high **performance** time keeping
Sportura – built for speed.
The world's only Kinetic Chronograph, with 4 separate dials to measure every increment of time and Kinetic technology that uses your body's energy to create electrical power, so there is no battery change - ever!
A breathtaking example of Seiko's forward thinking.
www.seiko.co.uk 01628 770988
SEIKO
forward **thinking**
SEIKO
RESET
START/STOP
Sportura
Sportura
KINETIC®
CHRONOGRAPH

16 Creating a Print Ad

OBJECTIVES TR10, TR11, SL7, SL12

- **To identify how media texts are tailored to suit their audience, and recognise that audience responses vary, e.g. *popular websites***
- **To recognise how print, sounds and still or moving images combine to create meaning**
- **To answer questions pertinently, drawing on relevant evidence or reasons**
- **To use exploratory, hypothetical and speculative talk as a way of researching ideas and expanding thinking**

In this lesson you will have the chance to write and design a print advertisement. Three stages of production will be involved: planning, development and evaluation.

STARTER

Memorable Slogans

A successful advertisement is usually one that people remember. One way to make people remember an advertisement is by using a good slogan that will stick in people's minds.

For each of the following products, think of a slogan that has been used to advertise it.

Mobile Phone: The future's bright. The future's Orange

Perfume:

Car:

Chocolate Bar:

Footwear:

Airlines: We'll take good care of you (BA)

Explain how each slogan works and why people are likely to remember it.

Share your ideas with the class.

INTRODUCTION

Knowing your Product

You are going to write and design a print advertisement for a new mobile phone. Start by reading the information on page 43. The image and print elements of the three phones have been jumbled.

Your task is first to match up these elements for your chosen product. You will need to select the an appropriate:

Product name	**Logo**
Image/illustration	**Shoutline**
Slogan	**Blurb**

Ensure that one member of the group records your decisions during this planning stage and be ready to explain your choices to the class.

Use a grid like the one below to draw up a profile of the target audience for your mobile:

Gender	Income
Age	Social Class

Finally, consider *why* you think that audience might be interested in your product. For example, to save them time, to make them seem more attractive to other people.

DEVELOPMENT

Developing Your Ad

PC

The next stage is for your group to design your print advertisement.

You will need to think carefully about how the different elements will work together.

- How much space will be given over to image?
- Will you use all the print elements?
- Would you use a different font?
- What other images or print elements would you include?

Plan out your advertisement on a plain sheet of A4 paper. Or use a photocopy and cut and paste the elements.

Consider how a reader will look at the page so that you can make sure that the most important information will catch his/her eye first.

Evaluate your final design by making notes on what has worked well and the elements that could be developed further.

Product name	Slogan	Shoutline	Blurb
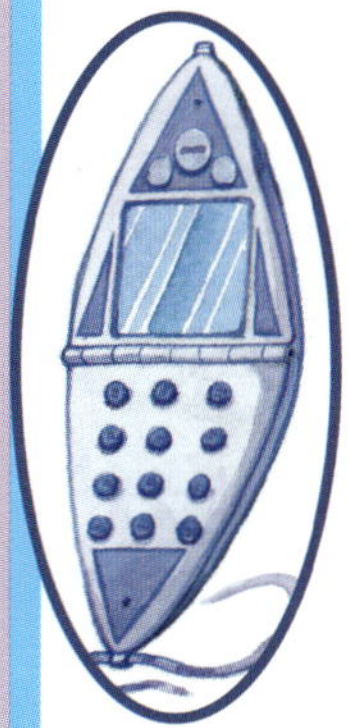 BT's E.T.	Singing in the rain? Laughing all the way to the bank?	You can take it anywhere: plane, car, train, boat or even tube.	Leave all your cares to Parker- With X* new intelligent 'Parker' chip, you really can stay in touch from anywhere in the world. You won't have to switch it off or redial, 'Parker' will do it for you.
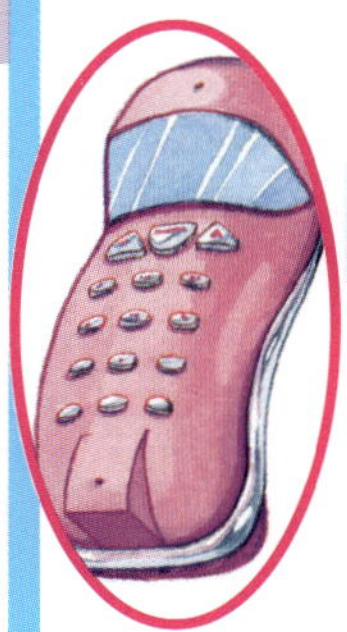 SAMS 200	'Yes milady, I really can be at your service 24/7.'	You can do all this and more.	Using the new X couldn't be easier with its compact shape, sharp images, ultra-fast texting that say even more…
 Fabfone	Phone anywhere Anytime Anyway	Add something EXTRA with Extra.Texting.	X is waterproof, shock proof and fast connecting with a dazzling 4.5 cm colour image, all you need to stay in touch and stay moving.

*Wherever you see X in the blurb, insert the name of your chosen product.

INFO

How We Read Ads

We tend to read an ad from the top left of the page across to the right and then downwards. However, we can also be 'guided' in how we 'read' by the construction of an ad. For example, the Samsung advertisement on page 39 encourages us to read from the centre right of the page first. The way the image is cropped and lit influences where we search for meaning first.

PLENARY

Display all the finished mobile phone advertisements.

Be prepared in your groups to use the notes you have made to feed back on one of the three stages of the advertisement's production.

17 What Girls Want

OBJECTIVES S9, TR2, TR9, TW17

- **To adapt the stylistic conventions of the main non-fiction text types to fit different audiences and purposes, e.g. *advertisements, documentaries, editorials***
- **To undertake independent research using a range of reading strategies, applying their knowledge of how texts and ICT databases are organised and acknowledging sources**
- **To recognise how texts are shaped by the technology they use, e.g. *the use of sound and image in computer animation***
- **To integrate evidence into writing, to support analysis and conclusions, e.g. *data, quotation***

In this lesson you will be looking at the ways in which magazines are products designed to suit their particular audience, using examples of magazines chiefly aimed at girls.

STARTER

What Interests Girls?

Working in groups of four, produce a list of the types of article girls are interested in reading. Pool information with all the girls in your class. List at least five items.

Now look at the cover and contents page of *Sugar* magazine opposite. Compare your list with the items covered by the magazine. Be ready to present your ideas to the rest of the class as a list headed 'What girls' magazines think girls are interested in'. How successful is the magazine in understanding girls' interests?

INFO

Magazine Research

Companies that produce girls' magazines target a small audience, i.e., girls between the ages of 9 and 13. This audience is identified through product research conducted by phone and questionnaire. Companies shape their magazines to attract this audience. The result is that these magazines often include conventional subjects and cover them in conventional ways.

INTRODUCTION

Getting their Attention

Look again at the magazine on page 45. How effective do you think the style of the cover and contents page is in attracting girls aged up to 13 for each of the following:

- Typography – how words look on the page
- Layout – the way the images and text are organised
- Teasers – items chosen to 'sell' the magazine
- Tone of the language
- Illustration
- Colour

DEVELOPMENT

Your Views

Now, using your discussion notes from the Starter and the Introduction, write a commentary on the magazine cover and contents list based on the writing frame below.

Begin by drafting the first paragraph as a class. Draw together the information from the Info Box and from your notes to give the following details:

Para 1

Explain HOW the front cover targets the audience.

Give precise examples of words and images used to support your comments.

Continue to use your notes to write paragraphs 2 and 3, using the writing frame that follows. Remember this is your chance to express your views on how particular magazines present girls' interests.

Para 2

Give general information about the magazine, e.g. title, cost, audience.

Compare what the class said girls are interested in with the topics flagged up on front cover of Sugar.

Para 3 - Your personal view

Explain what you would change about this cover and why.

PLENARY

Display your views on the classroom wall. Pairs should then browse over all the pieces and write one positive comment on a chosen piece of work and one suggestion for improvement.

Be prepared to explain your comments to the class.

18 Magazine Launch

OBJECTIVES S9, TW10, SL10

- **To adapt the stylistic conventions of the main non-fiction text types to fit different audiences and purposes, e.g. *advertisements, documentaries, editorials***
- **To organise and present information, selecting and synthesising appropriate material and guiding the reader clearly through the text, e.g. *a technological process, an information leaflet***

Extra Resources

Optional: Introduction and Development - several examples of magazines aimed at both boys and girls.

In this lesson you will look at how market information, such as readership data for magazines is used to ensure products meet their target audience.

STARTER

Readership Profiles

Look at the readership profile for *Top of the Pops* magazine below. This profile gives details of the type of people who have bought the magazine. This information is helpful to advertisers when they are deciding which magazine to use for their advertising campaign. Decide from the profile:

- Who is the main audience for *TOTP*?
- What is their average age?
- What is the readership figure for *TOTP*?
- How many copies sell every month?
- Who do you anticipate being the other 20% of the *TOTP* audience?

Having examined the readership profile in detail, predict what type of products might be advertised in *TOTP* and why. Create a class list of these.

INFO

Readership Profile

Data collected about the size and nature of readership is called a **readership profile**. This might be gathered by the publisher or by a market research company for the publisher. For example, the BBC reports that 244 thousand copies of *TOTP* are sold every month. Its readers are 80% female with an average age of 13. The estimated readership of *TOTP* magazine is 1.5 million.

INTRODUCTION

TOTP Teasers

The *TOTP* cover uses each of the features outlined in the grid below to target its audience. Make notes on each feature, using the information in the readership profile and the model below to guide you.

Cover feature	How it targets the audience
Title	The title itself and its typography is so well known to the target audience through the TV show that the BBC do not need to reveal the whole title, i.e. they can afford to overlap the image with it.
Headlines	
Typography	
Illustrations	
Teasers	
Layout	
Price	
Free gifts	

Be ready to share your findings with the rest of the class.

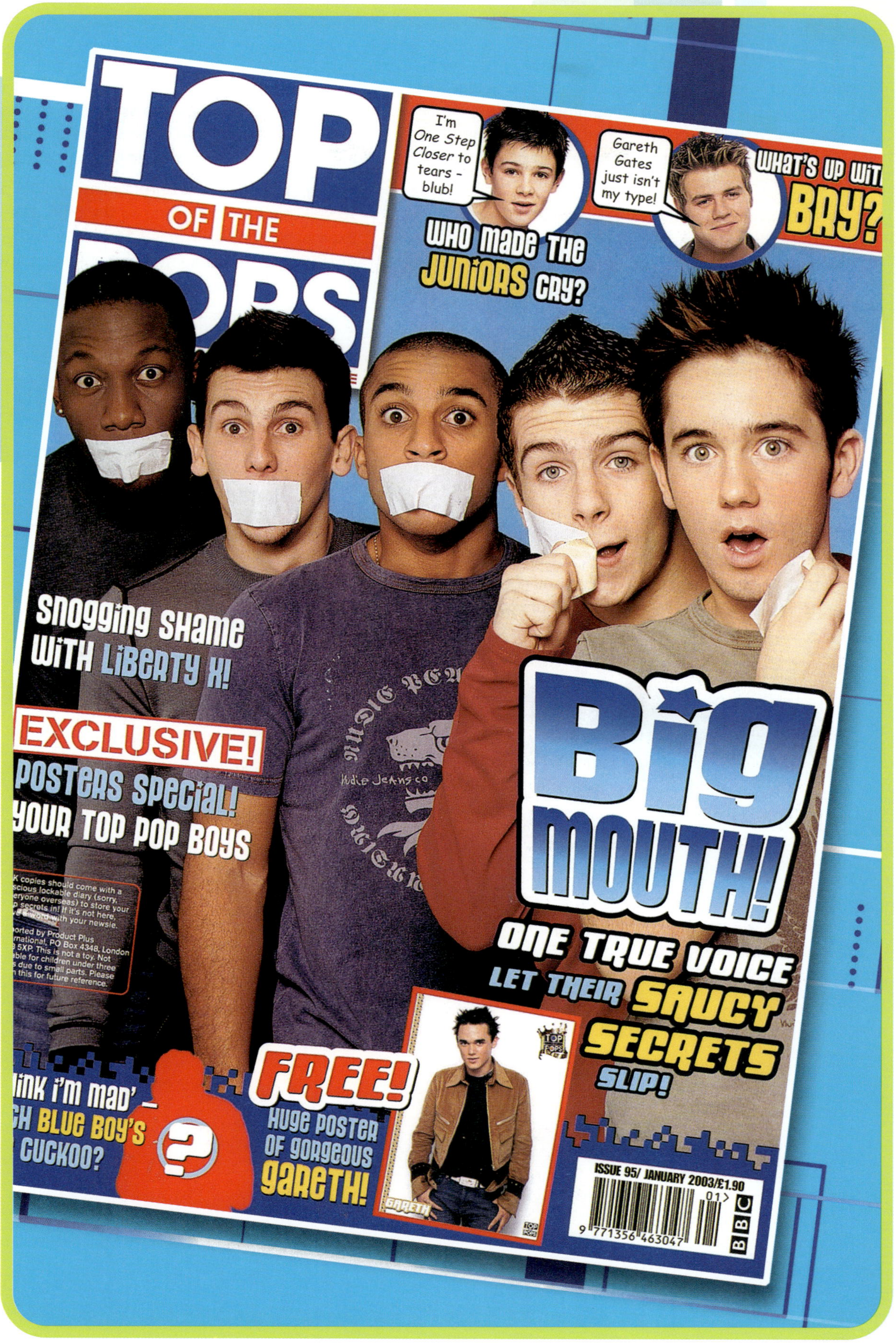
TOP OF THE POPS
I'm One Step Closer to tears – blub!
WHO MADE THE JUNIORS CRY?
Gareth Gates just isn't my type!
WHAT'S UP WITH BRY?
SNOGGING SHAME WITH LIBERTY X!
EXCLUSIVE!
POSTERS SPECIAL! YOUR TOP POP BOYS
Big MOUTH!
ONE TRUE VOICE LET THEIR SAUCY SECRETS SLIP!
FREE! HUGE POSTER OF GORGEOUS GARETH!
GARETH
CH BLUE BOY'S CUCKOO?
ISSUE 95/ JANUARY 2003/£1.90
BBC

DEVELOPMENT

Devising your Magazine

Working in the same groups, prepare a design proposal for a new magazine aimed at boys and girls of your age. You need to ensure that your magazine will be as different as possible from other magazines already on the market.

- Remember the audience is boys and girls below the age of 14
- Use your research into girls' interests and how these are targeted in magazines
- Brainstorm a list of boys' interests which might be included

Give your magazine a working title, one that suggests its stance on things. Then briefly comment on its characteristics under the following sub-headings:

- Visual style
- Content (subject matter)
- Written style

The two places that a magazine's image are most apparent are on the cover and the contents page. Add to your design proposal:

- A front cover design
- A draft contents page

Use the template on page 49 to remind you of the elements you need to include in the new cover. Discuss each element and note down ideas for your cover beneath each heading.

Finally, prepare a list of facts that will help you to sell this new magazine to the BBC. Use examples from your cover template and your draft contents list to support your argument. The model below will guide you.

Fact about the audience	Element in cover/contents that meets this
Boys make up 50% of audience	Photostory features action film stars

PLENARY

Each group should now present their new magazine proposal to the class in role as BBC publishers.

Explain your decisions clearly.

- How did you decide on the cover design?
- What type of content have you chosen?
- What attitude/image does the visual style display?
- What stance/tone does the text adopt?

title

Photo story introduced/names of two celebrities featured

Key articles flagged up

Main promotional photo

Caption for main photo

Mystery interview

Freebies + small photo/bar code/cost/publisher

19 Magazine Advice

OBJECTIVES S9, TW10, TW15

- **Adapt the stylistic conventions of the main non-fiction text types to fit different audiences and purposes, e.g. advertisements, documentaries, editorials**
- **Organise and present information, selecting and synthesising appropriate material and guiding the reader clearly through the text, e.g. *a technological process, an information leaflet***
- **To give written advice which offers alternatives and takes account of the possible consequences, e.g. *money management for young people***

In this lesson you will look at advice pages in magazines aimed at girls aged 9-13 and learn how to write one yourself.

STARTER

Tempting Titles

Girls' magazines specialise in giving advice to their readers on many different topics. They are tempted into reading this advice by titles that get their interest. Study the following headlines of advice pages and identify the language features that help to gain the reader's attention.

10 steps to happiness

Bathtime Bliss!

Top tips to Beat the Winter Blues

How to handle a scandle

Make yourself Bootyful

Use of imperative form and a current slang word

Make up one advice page headline on a health issue using language features identified above.

Be ready to share your titles as a class.

INTRODUCTION

What Makes Good Advice?

Now look carefully at the advice page 'How to be a perfect pal' on page 51. Give answers with examples to the following questions.

- What is the article about?
- What sort of headline has it got?
- What sort of reader do you think it is aimed at?
- What kinds of language does it use, e.g. rhetorical questions, the imperative
- Is there an illustration? What is its purpose?
- How does the intro line make you want to read more of the article?

DEVELOPMENT

Writing Advice

You are now going to plan and write an advice page for a teenage magazine. As a class, think of a topic that you think would make an advice page that is interesting to both girls and boys reading the magazine. Here are some ideas for topics:

- Fashion
- Sport
- Relationships
- Health and fitness

OHT Plan your article by coming up with section headings. An example for sport would be:

Section	Main focus
Intro line	What are the ways to excel in a sport?
1	Give tips on learning the basic skills
2	Give tips on practising these skills and improving
3	Give tips on the best equipment and round off

how to be a perfect pal!

Follow our top tips and you'll be the best mate ever!

- Why don't you make a birthday book? You can keep a list of all your friends' birthdays and that way you won't forget!
- If your mate's feeling a bit down why don't you cheer her up by organising a make-over session or sleepover especially for her?!
- If you see a picture of her fave celeb in a magazine then cut it out and keep it. It'll show that you've been thinking about her.
- Make sure you stick up for your mate if she's being bullied or someone's slagging her off. Imagine how you'd feel if she didn't stick up for you.
- Don't worry if you don't like all the same boys, clothes, music etc. It's good to know someone who likes different things to you – you'll be totally clued-up!
- Friendship bracelets are a fab way to show your mate how much you like her. You could make matching bracelets with your names on them as an extra-special treat for your mate!
- If she's always there for you as a shoulder to cry on then make sure you do the same whenever she needs to moan!
- If you've got a boyfriend and she hasn't, don't spend all your time speaking about him cos it'll make her feel left out.
- Don't get jealous of your friend's other mates. Try to talk to them too and join in cos more mates mean more FUN!
- Even if you speak all day at school and text each other all night, post her a letter or send her a card telling her why you think she's a great mate – it'll be a fab surprise!
- If she wants you to ask out a lad that she fancies cos she's too shy then you have to do it! If he says no, make sure you let her down gently and pretend you didn't like him anyway!
- If your mate tells you an important secret make sure you keep it a secret!

36

Write the introductory section together as a class. This should hook your reader in to read the rest of the advice.

Then write the second section in small groups on an OHT. Each group will then share their section 2 and the class will give suggestions for improving it.

Following your class plan, continue writing your advice page. Remember to give it an interesting headline.

Decide together what illustrations or photos you would include with your advice page.

When you have finished, exchange work with another group and review each other's writing. Use a different coloured pen and edit the writing carefully, considering these elements:

- Spelling
- Type of words used: adjectives, nouns
- Range of sentences: simple/complex, use of rhetorical questions and the imperative
- Style: humour/slang/formal/informal

PLENARY

Listen as two or three advice pages are read to the class. Explain briefly how you think each would appeal to the audience it has been written for.

Comment on any differences in style, and use of language and illustration.

20 Specialist Magazine Reviews

OBJECTIVES W12, W14, S12, *TW1*

- **To recognise how the degree of formality influences word choice**
- **To collect and comment on examples of language change, e.g. *new words associated with electronic communication and ICT***
- **To explore and use different degrees of formality in written and oral texts, e.g. *formal speeches, informal journal***

Extra Resources

Necessary: Development – a small selection of games from which to choose one to review.

In this section you will look at the sorts of technical language used in specialist magazines and in particular in computer game reviews.

INFO

REGISTER

The **register** of a text is the language that is appropriate in a particular set of circumstances. Language experts have suggested that a register has three dimensions:

- How technical it is
- How formal it is
- Whether it is spoken or written

STARTER

Register of Language

Read the review of the computer game *Shadow of Zorro* on page 53. Find examples of the three main features of the register of reviews as outlined below:

* Reasonably technical language, e.g. 'the classic PSI sneak 'em up'
* Reasonably informal language, e.g. 'Spidey and Batman wouldn't be too chuffed'
* Features of written style, e.g. complex sentences, 'Instead of real-time sword fighting, which you'd think would be a selling point of any Zorro game, the combat is handled in a rhythm action style...'

Consider what kinds of register might be appropriate for the following situations.

- Chatting with your parents about what you've done at school
- Talking to your friends about football/music
- Writing to your French pen-friend in French

Be ready to share your ideas with the class.

INTRODUCTION

What Makes it 'Male'?

Both the reviews on page 53 are from a computer magazine with a largely male readership. What do you notice about the language used? Make a note of the following:

- Technical words, phrases or acronyms that the reader might not understand without knowing about computers/computer games
- Informal words or phrases and/or in-jokes
- Words that indicate the audience is more likely to be male

Be prepared to explain your findings.

DEVELOPMENT

Drafting a Review

Drawing on the notes made during the Introduction, the class is going to draft a computer game review.

First brainstorm a list of games or use the selection the class have brought in. It may help to sort them into 'genres', e.g. Sports, Strategy, 'Shoot-em-up', Sims, etc. Decide as a class which game you will review.

As a class write the first paragraph of your review on the board/OHT.

In pairs, write the second paragraph. You should be prepared to read this out so that the whole class can consider it.

TICKER TAPE

Speedball is back, and it's gone all *Quake*. Just as we were going to press the Bitmap Brothers announced a new game in their venerated future sports series, *Speedball Arena*. Using cutting edge FPS technology, the game will bring the familiar brutality of the classic *Speedball* to online multiplayer gaming. We'll take a better look at the game next issue, in the meantime check out www.speedballarena.com

SHADOW OF ZORRO

According to our hosts in Paris, Zorro is the second most widely known fictional hero in the world, after Superman. How they came to this unlikely conclusion we can't be certain, but we imagine Spidey and Batman wouldn't be too chuffed to hear about it, not to mention Lara and Mario. Unfortunately for Zorro his first ever computer game is unlikely to push him into the number one spot, as it's looking utterly abysmal. It's basically a swashbuckling rip-off of the classic PS1 sneak 'em up *Tenchu: Stealth Assassins*, with a few elements inexpertly nicked from *Metal Gear Solid* and other stealthy hits. Which wouldn't be so bad if it didn't look second-rate in every department, and boast one of the worst combat systems ever devised. Instead of real-time sword fighting, which you'd think would be a selling point of any Zorro game, the combat is handled in a rhythm action style, wherein you must mimic a series of key combinations flashed up on the screen to perform each sword strike. If successful you get to watch a cut-scene of Zorro parrying and thrusting with customary aplomb. If not, you see another cut-scene of the enemy making a fool of him. Stupid, stupid, stupid.

Now complete the review working in your pair. You could follow the writing frame opposite.

PLENARY

Listen as a number of the computer game reviews are read to the class.

Display your computer game reviews on the classroom wall. With your partner select one review. Suggest two ways to improve it. Use a different coloured pen and make the changes.

Decide which review you found most persuasive. Give two reasons why.

Para 1 Give details of title/company/format/cost/unique selling point (USP)

Para 2 Expand on USP with detail from the game, e.g. quality of graphics/ degree of difficulty/special features/speed of action/two player or one/level of interactivity

Para 3 Compare the game to its rivals.

Para 4 Give personal example of/anecdote about playing

Para 5 Recommend whether to buy the game. Give reasons and a score out of 10

21 Bigstar.com

OBJECTIVES W14, *TR3*, TR8, TR9

- **To collect and comment on examples of language change, e.g. *new words associated with electronic communication and ICT***
- **To investigate how meanings are changed when information is presented in different forms or transposed into different media.**
- **To recognise how texts are shaped by the technology they use, e.g. *the use of sound and image in computer animation***

In this lesson you will explore some of the information available on the Internet about Hollywood stars.

STARTER

Describing the Stars

The words in the list below are often used to describe film stars. Brainstorm what you think each word means in this context. Use a dictionary to help you.

Hunk	Prima Donna
Troubled	Mega
Babe	A' list
Oscar winner	Maverick

Discuss your ideas on each word as a class.

INTRODUCTION

Web Page Conventions

Look at website 2 opposite. Compare the features of a webpage and a magazine page. Use a grid like the one below to make your comparison:

Layout Feature	Webpage	Magazine
Use of headings	Actor/ Character profile info	
Language	informal	
Use of colour		
Typography		
Illustrations		
Links		

Summarise in three sentences what you think are the main conventions of a webpage.

DEVELOPMENT

Different Views of Elijah

Now read website pages 1 and 2 shown on page 55. They are both devoted to Hollywood star, Elijah Wood. One is the official *Lord of the Rings* website with information produced on behalf of the star. The other is an unofficial site produced by a fan of Elijah's. In groups, give examples of features from the two sites. Use a grid like the one below.

Fansite feature	Website 1	Websi
Navigation buttons - that link to other parts of website		
Images		
Formal interview text		
Biographical info		
Interactive links		

Also make notes on the tone and language used to address the reader on these sites. Find examples of these features and explain their use.

- Spoken register (dialogue)
- Third person or first person?
- Past tense
- Simple sentences
- Note-form text

Be ready to explain the differences in tone between the two websites.

PLENARY

Feed back on the similarities and differences between the two websites.

Which website was more interesting and why?

1

Back Forward Stop Refresh Home AutoFill Print Mail

Address: http://www.lordoftherings.net/index_101_fi_excl.html

HOME

CAST ELIJAH WOOD BILLY BOYD DOMINIC MONAGHAN SEAN ASTIN IAN MCKELLEN IAN

Filmmakers Pr

ON THE SET

INTERVIEW WITH ELIJAH WOOD – PART ONE

CLICK HERE FOR BIO

Below is an on the set interview with Elijah Wood, who stars as the hobbit Frodo Baggins, during the filming of The Lord of the Rings in New Zealand.

Part One

"My name is Elijah Wood and I'm Frodo Baggins."

Q: What's it like in New Zealand?

EW: I'll tell you what it's like in New Zealand. New Zealand is gorgeous. It's so beautiful and with this project, we've been able to travel around and we're going to continue to travel to various locations and many places that people don't normally get to see, so that's been really great.

Q: How do you think the landscape of New Zealand compares to Middle-earth?

EW: That's actually the first thing I thought when Peter showed me all the pictures and things of the locations … this is Middle-earth. I mean it has every sort of geographical, geological formation, landscape, it's got everything, you know. So, it's absolutely perfect for New Zealand.

2

elijah-wood.com – The Elijah Wood Fan Network...

Back Forward Stop Refresh Home AutoFill Print Mail

Address: http://www.elijah-wood.com/english/index.php

Index

Home News About Elijah Movies & TV Multimedia Interactive Shopping

FAQs

PERSONAL DETAILS

Full Name – Elijah Jordan Wood
Nicknames – Monkey, The Funny, Elwood, and 'Lij
Date of Birth – January 28, 1981
Place of Birth – Cedar Rapids, Iowa, USA
Religion – Christian
Nationality – American
Occupation – Actor
Height – 5'6" (168cm)
Weight – 163lbs
Eyes – Blue
Hair – Dark Brown
Education – Enrolled in modelling school at Avant Studios in Cedar Rapids
Relationship – does not have a girlfriend, last girlfriend: German actor Franka Potente
Currently Lives – Los Angeles, California< USA
Currently Drives – Red Ferrari
Parents – Warren Wood and Deborah Wood
Siblings – Older brother Zachariah and younger sister Hannah
Pets – 2 dogs, Rascal and Levonne
Hobbies – Photography, Reading, fencing, in-line skating, swimming, basketball, hockey, cooking and singing
Collects – Star Wars figures
Smokes – Clove Cigarettes
Tattoo – On the lower right-side of his torso, Wood has been branded with a 3-inch tattoo, a strange series of croocked, vertical lines that looks like a wrapped product bar. "It's Elvish," Wood says, "It stands for the number nine."

FAVOURITES

Band – Beatles and Smashing Pumpkins
CD's – Mellon Collie and The Infinite Sadness –(S.P)
Color – Blue
Food – Homemade potato salad
Movies – The Star Wars Trilogy, Heavenly Creatures, and Braveheart
Worst Movie – Godzilla
Actor – Tim Roth
Actress – Emma Thompson
Subject in School – English
Books – Victor Hugo's The Hunchback of Notre Dame, and The Hobbit by J.R.R. Tolkien
TV Shows – Entertainment Weekly and Extra
Sport – In-line Skating

Internet zone

22 Attracting an Audience

OBJECTIVES W14, *TR3*, TR8, TR9

- To collect and comment on examples of language change, e.g. *new words associated with electronic communication and ICT*
- To investigate how meanings are changed when information is presented in different forms or transposed into different media.
- To recognise how texts are shaped by the technology they use, e.g. *the use of sound and image in computer animation*

In this lesson you will look at how print texts communicate to us by focusing on film posters.

STARTER

Cinema Experiences

Take each word in the list below and brainstorm what you understand and associate with it. Use the model for Certificate to guide you.

Movie
Screen
Multiplex
Certificate, e.g. standard, legal age, permission, excitement
Box Office
Premiere
Digital sound

INTRODUCTION

Analysing the Poster

Posters, like the one on page 57 for *Star Wars The Attack of the Clones,* are carefully designed to **market** a product and to have maximum impact on their audiences.

Discuss in your group the reasons why people would want to see this film. For example:

- Science fiction genre
- Special effects
- Sequel
- Characters
- Director

Now look at how the poster persuades you to go and see the film. Identify the most persuasive features of the Star Wars poster. Consider the following elements and make a note of how each makes an impact on the reader.

- Images
- Title
- Graphics
- Typography
- Star names

Discuss whether the persuasive features of the poster match the reasons you identified for going to see the film.

DEVELOPMENT

Designing a Film Poster

Here are some storylines for films that might be released at the cinema. You are going to select one and design a poster to advertise it.

- Comedy - A baby is stolen mistakenly by robbers. Local kid (a geek) knows how to get baby back
- Romance - Two young people of different religions/ ethnic backgrounds fall in love. Parents disagree, the kids run away
- Drama - A young man drifts into crime/gang life. He wants out and has to turn traitor to save himself and his family

Spend a few minutes fleshing out the storyline you have chosen. Try to come up with a story that contains the five stages of narrative:

Introduction,
Development,
Complication,
Crisis,
Resolution.

Now map out and plan a film poster for the plot you have developed. Your plan should show where the following elements would go:

- The title of the film
- Details of the 'star' names
- A shoutline to draw readers' attention
- Quotes from reviews
- Graphics/images from the film
- Date for release of film in cinemas near you?

Remember you are aiming for maximum persuasive effect.

PLENARY

Display all the posters on the walls. Decide which film you would go to see and say which parts of the poster persuaded you.

23 Reviewing Films

OBJECTIVES W14, TR6, TW14

- To collect and comment on examples of language change, e.g. *new words associated with electronic communication and ICT*
- To recognise bias and objectivity, distinguishing facts from hypotheses, theories or opinions
- To develop and signpost arguments in ways that make the logic clear to the reader

Extra Resources

Optional: Introduction and Development – current film reviews and cinema listings for consideration.

In this lesson you will learn about film reviews and get the chance to write one yourself.

STARTER

Summing up Film Types

Look at these quotes from film reviews. Explain briefly what each one means and think of a film for which it might be an appropriate description. Follow the model below:

An absolute turkey – the phrase refers to a film that is really awful and that will fail. The turkey, as a literal reference, is doomed to die and figuratively the film will do the same thing. Also the noun 'turkey' refers to a comic image so the film is also being mocked because it is so bad.

- *A slick action-packed thriller*
- *A suspense thriller that really grips*
- *A real weepie*
- *A masterpiece of modern cinema*
- *Keeps you on the edge of your seat*

Can you think of other phrases to sum up a film? Be ready to share your views.

INTRODUCTION

Fact and Opinion

Listen as review 1 of *The Wild Thornberry's Movie* is read to you. It is taken from *The Observer* newspaper review section. Then work together to write two lists: one noting the facts about the film in the review, the other noting the opinions. Discuss how you can tell the difference.

Now compare the two lists. Which list is the longer? Why is this?

Do you think this review is useful to someone trying to decide if they should see the film? Does the writer have a good sense of the target audience for the film?

With a partner, read review 2 of *The Wild Thornberry's*, taken from the Channel 4 Teletext service. Again make two lists - one of the facts in the review and the other of the opinions. Be ready to share your findings with the class.

DEVELOPMENT

Writing your Film Review

Decide on a current film that you would like to review. Choose from a cinema listing if necessary. The review should be about 70 words long and include brief details of:

- The plot
- The characters
- Any special effects or features
- Your opinions on all the above

The language features of film reviews are those of both persuasive and informative texts, so try and use most of the following:

- *Present tense, e.g. The father has a handlebar moustache*
- *Complex sentences – sometimes beginning with the subordinate clause, e.g. With its rudimentary animation...*
- *Lists of three, e.g. with Brenda Blethyn. Rupert Everett and Marisa Tomei taking parts*
- *Expanded noun phrases, e.g. a jolly Anglo-American family*
- *Emotive language, e.g. there's not much here even for...*

Above all, remember to consider who the audience might be for your film.

1

The film is overlong, the music s… melodramatic, but the central performances ar… affecting and the underlying social criticism fairly sharp.

The Wild Thornberrys Movie, a spin-off from an animated TV series, is a surprisingly entertaining story of a jolly Anglo-American family making wildlife documentaries in Africa. The father has a handlebar moustache and a parodic Bertie Wooster accent (courtesy of Tim Curry), his younger daughter has been given the gift of speaking to animals, and the family pet is a smart monkey called Darwin. Their enemies are a pair of European poachers, who kill cheetahs for their skins and elephants for their tusks and are brought to book by the native police. The film's draughtsmanship is more than adequate, the voicing of the characters excellent, and the songs are way above the average for such fare.

In **F… Destination 2**, directed by David R. Ellis, a … action films,

2

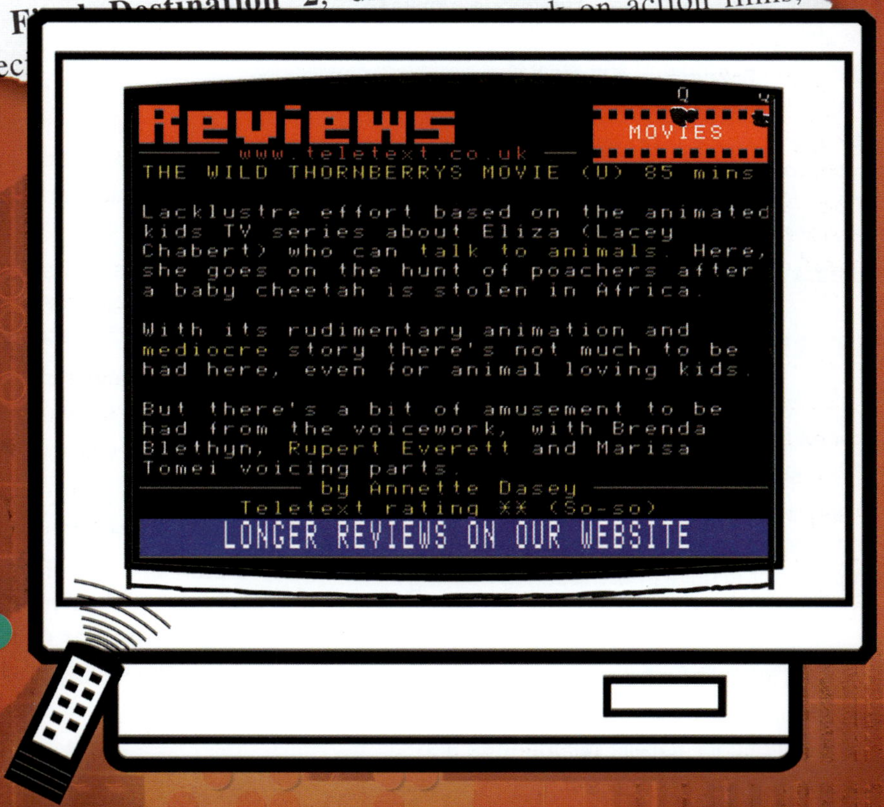

Reviews

MOVIES

www.teletext.co.uk

THE WILD THORNBERRYS MOVIE (U) 85 mins

Lacklustre effort based on the animated kids TV series about Eliza (Lacey Chabert) who can talk to animals. Here, she goes on the hunt of poachers after a baby cheetah is stolen in Africa.

With its rudimentary animation and mediocre story there's not much to be had here, even for animal loving kids.

But there's a bit of amusement to be had from the voicework, with Brenda Blethyn, Rupert Everett and Marisa Tomei voicing parts.

by Annette Dasey

Teletext rating ** (So-so)

LONGER REVIEWS ON OUR WEBSITE

PLENARY

Listen as some of the film reviews are read to the class.

Think carefully about how effectively the writer has used the language features listed on page 58.

Decide whether each review has persuaded you to see or rent the film.

24 Film Information

OBJECTIVES TR6, TR8, TW16

- To recognise bias and objectivity, distinguishing facts from hypotheses, theories or opinions
- To investigate how meanings are changed when information is presented in different forms or transposed into different media
- To weigh different viewpoints and present a balanced analysis of an event or issue, e.g. *an environmental issue or historical investigation*

In this lesson you will explore the different ways in which information about a film is made available to potential viewers.

STARTER

Examining Sources

Brainstorm where you get your information about up-coming or current films. Think about different media sources, such as newspapers, magazines, radio, television, telephone info line and website. List these and then next to each one write an example of the sort of information you would expect to find.

television - review on Saturday Show - opinions about the film and basic facts; trailer for film - dramatic scenes and dates for release

Feed back your ideas to the class.

INTRODUCTION

Getting at the Information

First look at the cinema listing on page 61 for films being shown at a cinema multiplex.

Working with a partner, write down the types of information you can obtain from these listings. What crucial information is missing from the listing? Which other text on page 61 contains this?

Using your own knowledge of the titles in the listing, decide on the genre of six of the films. Use the certificate details to judge the age range of the audience.

Follow the example below.

e.g. Solaris sounds like a science fiction film aimed at teenagers and adults.

Decide between you which of the listed films you would most like to see.

Be ready to share your findings with the class.

DEVELOPMENT

Planning a Radio Review

You are going to prepare a short radio review of the film you would most like to see from current listings.

The review will:

- Only last 30 seconds
- Use a tone appropriate for its target audience
- Use some of the language features of reviews listed on page 58
- Include facts and opinions about your chosen film

Make some notes for your review and then place them in the order that will have most impact on the listener.

Now turn your notes into short prompts on a prompt card, like the one on page 61.

If possible record your review.

PLENARY

Listen as some of the radio reviews are played or read. Make a note of which one you think would work best on radio and why.

Think of one way in which you might improve the delivery of your own review.

Odeon

Maid in Manhattan (PG), Far From Heaven (12A), The Pianist (15), Jackass (18), Analyze That (15), Solaris (12A), The Ring (15), Chicago (12A), Wild Thornberry's (U), Two Weeks Notice (12A), Treasure Planet (U), Catch Me If You Can (12A). Sat/Sun Lord of the Rings, The Two Towers (12A), Harry Potter and the Chamber of Secrets (PG). Fri/Sat/Sun Spy Kids 2 (U), Men in Black 2 (PG), The Powderpuff Girls (U). Sun/Mon Khushi (12A). Wed senior screen My Big Fat Greek Wedding (PG). Thurs 13/3 The Life of David Gale (15).

0870 5050007

Odeon

That (15), Solaris (12A), The Ring (15), Chicago

<u>Chicago</u>

- Nominated for a whole host of Oscars, including one for Catherine Zeta Jones, as best supporting actress
- Set in 1920s Chicago, the plot mixes showbiz with social issues
- Characters Velma Kelly (Zeta Jones) and Roxie Hart (Zellweger) are both in jail accused of murdering their partners
- Velma's a singer in a slinky nightclub; Roxie is a showbiz wannabe.
- Questions set up - Will lawyer, Billy Flynn, prove their only hope of escaping the death penalty?
- Great songs - All that Jazz - sets and costumes
- Plenty of pace and energy
- Opens in cinemas next Friday

25 Analysing Radio News

OBJECTIVES W14, TR9, SL9

- **To collect and comment on examples of language change, e.g. *new words associated with electronic communication and ICT***
- **To recognise how texts are shaped by the technology they use, e.g. *the use of sound and image in computer animation***
- **To discuss and evaluate conflicting evidence to arrive at a considered opinion**

Extra Resources

Necessary: Introduction and Development – three taped radio news bulletins from local, national and world service stations, representing both commercial and public service.

In this lesson you will learn about radio news bulletins and consider how they are put together.

STARTER

Radio Terms

Here are some terms used to describe the main features of a radio news bulletin. First look at the annotated script on page 63 to see examples of some of these features, then write a brief explanation for each one.

- Headline
- Report
- Interview/Comment
- Newsreader
- News item
- Actuality

Be prepared to share your explanations with the class.

INTRODUCTION

Where's the Listener?

Listen as each of the three news bulletins are played to you. Say which type of station you think each bulletin has come from: local, national or international. Use a grid like the one below to summarise evidence from the bulletins to support your decisions.

News bulletin features	Station A is...
News items included	
Choice of headline	
Speaking voice of news reader	
Use of language	
Length of bulletin	
Jingle for station	

What can you tell about the audience for each station from listening to the news bulletins?

Share your conclusions with the class.

INFO

News Values

News reporting in different media places emphasis on different types of story. For example, one possible set of news values might be: 1 loss of life, 2 natural disaster, 3 national politics, 4 issues of morality. Whereas another set might be: 1 loss of life, 2 natural disaster, 3 celebrity news, 4 national politics.

DEVELOPMENT

Reflecting News Values

Listen carefully to one of the bulletins again and write down the order in which the news items are presented. After each item decide what type of news you think it is:

- Local
- National
- International
- Entertainment
- Sport
- Business

Why do you think the items have been placed in this order, i.e. what are the **news values**?

Do you think the first story is more important than the last? How is this shown? Consider:

- The duration of the item
- Language/tone of the presenter
- Interviews/comments from people involved
- Information or sound recorded at the scene of the story. (This is called **actuality**.)

The example script on page 63 will help you identify these news features. (Note it does not show actuality.)

MERCURY NEWS 8 A.M. NEWS BULLETIN

*****

Release or try him....

THAT's the call over CROYDON Al-quaida suspect Feroz Abbassi ....

He's been held in Camp X-ray in Cuba for over a year now....

Newsreader delivers linking script

His MP Gerraint Davies sez action must be taken:

[play 12 second cut – phono]

'..it's important that evidence against him is put against him, that he's charged and punished appropriately and if there isn't any evidence and he's simply being held there for information, he's been there now a year and it's about time, er, he was, er, re-patriated to Britain.'

Clip from phone interview with MP concerned

[cut ends]

******

Gatwick's continuing to recover from September 11th.

The number of passengers travelling thru the aiport last month was nearly 6 per cent higher than February last year.

*****

A woman's been taken to hospital with serious injuries after a house fire in WHYTLEAFE....

The blaze on Hillbury Road severely damaged the ground floor...

The woman's being treated in the Mayday hospital in CROYDON...

News item

******

Women still aren't getting a good deal over pay.....

Headline

Two thirds actually get less than the average wage according to a new report...

A study for the TUC Women's Conference also sez a lack of childcare which women can afford is condemning them to poverty.

******

PLENARY

Listen as groups give their feedback on the local, national or international radio bulletin they focused on.

Discuss together the main audience for the different stations and their news values as represented in each news bulletin.

26 Writing Radio News

OBJECTIVES TR8, TR9, TW10, SL9

- **To investigate how meanings are changed when information is presented in different forms or transposed into different media**
- **To recognise how texts are shaped by the technology they use, e.g. *the use of sound and image in computer animation***
- **To organise and present information selecting appropriate material and guiding the reader clearly through the text, e.g. *technological process, an information leaflet***
- **To discuss and evaluate conflicting evidence to arrive at a considered opinion**

In this lesson you will have a chance to write your own radio news bulletin.

STARTER

Ear-grabbing Headlines

Like newspaper headlines, radio bulletin headlines are used as a 'hook' to grab the audience's attention.

They are often written in an abbreviated form to make them sound urgent and important.

They also sum up the event by answering some of the questions Where, What, Why, When and How?

Take each of the headlines below and write it out as a full sentence, like this:

An explosion in a factory in Peru has killed 57 people.

Then try to explain how each headline works. The following questions should help you with this.

- Are there are any verbs? What tense is used?
- What effect does the headline have if it is not written in standard English?

A **FACTORY EXPLOSION IN PERU KILLS 57 PEOPLE**

B **Spice Girls to play come back concert**

C **Manchester City demoted**

D **MOTORWAY PILE-UP**
ONE KILLED DOZENS INJURED

E **Fishing to be banned**

F Petrol price falls by 2p a litre

Be ready to share your notes with the class.

INTRODUCTION

Creating the Running Order

Choose five events in your school from the past few months which would provide good headlines for a bulletin on a school radio station.

Now decide in which order you will place the five stories to give maximum impact and to ensure the listener keeps listening. This is called a **running order**. It will be influenced by your **news values**. Your bulletin will last two minutes so allocate times against each item to fill this timeslot. Use the example below to guide you.

- *School to close and reopen as City Academy [30 seconds]*
- *Year 9 win national poetry competition [30 seconds]*
- *Integrating disabled students into our school [20 seconds]*
- *Break-in and theft during half term [20 seconds]*
- *Head of Science is to appear in local panto [20 seconds]*

DEVELOPMENT

Drafting the Script

Each choose one item from your running order which you will script. On your own, decide:

- What content you will include in your item
- If you will link to interviews inside and beyond the studio
- If you will link to actuality (material recorded on location)
- How you will script what the newsreader and reporter will say
- How you will keep to the time limit
- How you will link to the next item

[Title: Smoking Add on 1]
[For: Time: 8 a.m. Date: 11 Mar]

[Duration: Text: 17" Audio: 13" Total: 29"]

Are you giving up this no smoking day?

There's help, if you want to kick the habit in Surrey.

You can get group or one-to-one support as well as trying nicotine patches or anti-smoking drug, Zyban.

Emma Whitehead, from Mid Surrey Primary Care trust, sez support is very important...

"If people don't have support or don't use nicotine replacement therapy they're less likely to be able to...to succeed qu...quitting on their own but with ...with the help of ..er the support services the rate of quitting is greatly increased"

Audio: Duration: 13"
Outcue: increased

******

[Title: Corrie Add on ?]
[For: Time: 8 a.m. Date: 11 Mar]

[Duration: Text: 16" Total: 16"]

Millions are expected to tune in tonight to watch Corrie's Tricky Dicky meet a gruesome end.

The serial killer's given the soap its biggest viewing figures in years, but this evening his reign of terror finally finishes.

Dicky will be seen driving Gail and her children into a canal in a bid to kill them all.

It's not known who survives!

*****

Running Order

Mercury News bulletin 8a.m. 11 March

1 US backtracks on taking on Iraq alone
2 MP asks for Croydon man in Cuba's camp X-ray to be tried or released
3 Gatwick airport passenger figures rise
4 Housefire in Whytleafe
5 TUC Conference on Women's unfair rate of pay
6 Teenagers face fines for anti-social behaviour
7 Anti-smoking day – help available
8 Soap news – Corrie
9 Local football news
10 Weather

Now draft the script, using the script example above as a model. Remember to match the language and tone used to your school audience.

INFO

News Scripts

The Mercury News script on this page is written for a radio news bulletin. The newsreader has made small changes to the script before going on-air, so that it reads fluently and to show emphasis. The time allocation for each item is also marked on the script. The running order shows all the stories featured in the bulletin.

Rehearse the full script ensuring that the links between all five items work. Then tape your five-minute bulletin. Have your tape and running order ready to share with the class.

PLENARY

As you listen to each bulletin, note down:

- How well it targets the school audience, e.g. does it use an appropriate tone and language?
- How varied the items were, i.e. did they include interviews and actuality?
- How well the items linked to make a balanced bulletin, e.g. how do the tape and the running order compare?

27 Analysing Factual Radio

OBJECTIVES TR9, TW16, SL10

- **To recognise how texts are shaped by the technology they use, e.g. *the use of sound and image in computer animation***
- **To weigh different view points and present a balanced analysis of an event or issue, e.g. *an environmental issue or historical investigation***
- **To use talk to question, hypothesise, speculate, evaluate, solve problems and develop thinking about complex issues and ideas**

Extra Resources

Necessary: Starter – a five-minute taped clip of a talk radio programme. A studio discussion would work best.

In this lesson you will explore some of the demands of writing factual material for radio. You will be asked to research and write a documentary piece for a local radio station relating to issues relevant to your age group.

STARTER

Talk, Talk, Talk

Brainstorm a list of different types of talk radio. Use the examples below as a guide.

* Phone-ins
* Guest interviews

Decide which of these types are popular with your class.

Research suggests that there is not much interest in 'Talk radio' among people aged 11-16. This has been explained by:

- Competition from other media (such as the internet or digital television)
- A wider decline in the interest of 'young people' in serious factual issues.
- The style of these programmes being unfriendly to the age group.

Discuss whether you think these points are true for your class.

Listen to a clip from a speech-based programme recorded from the radio.

Using examples from the clip, work in pairs to produce lists under the headings in the grid above. One answer has been given for each to start you off.

Why 'Talk radio' may not appeal to me/my class	Subjects I would be interested in on the radio
I prefer to listen to music and watch talk shows for arguments	My rights: work/pay

Be prepared to share your views with the rest of the class.

INTRODUCTION

Choosing the Format

Imagine you have been asked by BBC youth programming to devise a factual radio programme aimed at 11 to 14 year olds.

First, think about the format of the programme you heard in the clip earlier. As a class, brainstorm a list of its main features, i.e. the content and style of the programme, how it is presented and how it involves the audience.

Work in a group of four to create a format for this new radio programme. You will need to address the questions that follow:

- What will it be called?
- When will it go on air? (i.e. day, time)
- How long will it be?
- How will it be presented?

The Moral Maze – Celebrity

Michael Buerk: What we are interested in is celebrity, those who are somehow famous for being famous, building them up, and better by far, pulling them down… Who should we expect to be good and why? That is our 'Moral Maze', live tonight.

Our panel, Professor Steven Rose, Director of the Brain and Behaviour Laboratory, Professor Ian Hargreaves Media Academic, Claire Fox from The Institute of Ideas and Michael Gove from *The Times*.

Michael Gove, what do you think today's celebrities represent?

Michael Gove: I think celebrities are there primarily to provide us with entertainment, and they can also act as living metaphors for lust or anger or greed in whatever sort of ethical discussion occupies the likes of us. In both respects they are the modern equivalents of Homeric* or Wagnerian** gods and as with Homer or Wagner, I find these characters' actions gripping - pure entertainment.

Michael Buerk: Steven Rose?

Steven Rose: Well, I would agree with Mike if they had some sort of moral worth or they were heroes in the Wagnerian sense. But without such worth, without heroism or any sense of virtue they are indeed famous for being famous, and I suppose that if you live by celebrity you will die by celebrity. I'm a little more troubled about this strange definition of the public interest which is operating here. Public interest isn't a high-minded thing, it's more what the public is interested in, it sells newspapers.

Michael Buerk: Claire Fox?

Claire Fox: What I'm more worried about is how today's confessional culture makes people famous for revealing their private lives, and the obsession with celebrities' private lives is very worrying, and does represent, as Steven just said, a loss of real heroes. A loss of respect for substantial achievement because we are more obsessed with character and lifestyle. Even more worrying, politicians are queuing up to become celebrities.

Michael Buerk: Ian Hargreaves?

Ian Hargreaves: Well I think celebrities are magnified and mass-communicated, so the idea that we expect some different kind of moral standard from them is logically and morally absurd.

Michael Buerk: Panel, thank you very much indeed. Our first witness is Mariella Fostrup, who is the thinking man's celebrity, of course! Mariella, how cynical, in your view is the world that creates and destroys celebrities like John Leslie and Angus Deaton.

Mariella Fostrup: Well, I suppose in my experiences of the music business and television, and journalism to an extent, and I think it is quite hilarious that we imagine that any of these businesses are infused with people bursting with moral fibre. I found the situation with Angus Deaton particularly ridiculous – he is the presenter of a comedy show and for the general public to perceive him as some sort of moral guide is utterly ridiculous.

*Homeric – with the same qualities as the characters in Homer's epic poem *The Iliad*.
** Wagnerian – with the same moral qualities as characters in operas by Wagner.

- What style will it adopt to maintain the audience's interest? (e.g. documentary, anarchic, educational, etc.)

Make notes of your reasons for these decisions. Producing written reasons is formally called a rationale. Use this way of presenting your reasoning.

We think that__________________________
because__________________________, for example__________________________.

DEVELOPMENT

Producing the Pilot

BBC youth programming is interested in your ideas and have asked you to make a pilot lasting no longer than ten minutes.

Working in your 'team', complete the following tasks.

- Identify two issues or topics to be covered. (You could use the headlines opposite to spark your ideas.)
- Identify three sources of information for each story (e.g. interviews, statistics, market research, Internet)
- Compile a research dossier for each story (a folder containing relevant information to be presented).
- Script the ten-minute pilot, dividing it so that each group member has the opportunity to write a segment. There should be an opportunity for arguments to be put on both sides for both topics. There will also need to be some linking text between the arguments and for the top and tail of the programme. (It will help you to refer back to the extract from *The Moral Maze* on page 67.)
- Include elements to draw the listener into the debate via text messaging, e-mail or phone vote responses.
- Record the pilot, checking on the accuracy of your timing.

Swap tapes with another group and listen to their recording. Assess how well they have formatted their pilot show under these headings:

- Features that appeal to the 11 to 14 age range
- Content of issues presented
- Style of presentation
- Interactive features

Be ready to share your assessment with the rest of the class.

PLENARY

Each group should present the rationale for its programme and then play its tape to the class.

Then the assessing groups, in role as BBC programmers, should give their feedback on each pilot.

Make a whole class list of the features and approaches that worked best in the pilots produced.

PARENTS TARGETED IN TRUANCY CRACKDOWN
Battle to cut teenage pregnancy rate
Football hooligan 'generals' jailed
JUNK FOOD STILL SERVED UP AT SCHOOL
REALITY TV IS HERE TO STAY
POLICE HIT AT RAPPERS FOR MAKING GUNS GLAMOROUS

28 Adapting for Radio

OBJECTIVES TR8, TR9, TW8

- **To investigate how meanings are changed when information is presented in different forms or transposed into different media.**
- **To recognise how texts are shaped by the technology they use, e.g. *the use of sound and image in computer animation***
- **To develop an imaginative or unusual treatment of familiar material or established conventions, e.g. *updating traditional tales***

In this section you will be looking at how stories can be adapted into scripts for other media, in this case radio.

STARTER

Playscript Language

There are certain language features that change when a story is adapted to a radio script.

- The story is written in the past tense, whereas script uses present tense to describe events in directions and in speech.
- Direct and indirect speech in the story has to be stripped down to the words of the characters in the script version.

Read the first two paragraphs of *The Daughter of the Sea* and rewrite two pieces of description as directions and two of indirect speech as the words of Ishmael or his wife. Follow the examples given below:

Story version	Script version
All the village fishermen who went out in boats returned with nets full.	(Sounds of fishing boats as they return to harbour)
How they laughed, and how he cursed.	(Sounds of men laughing) Fisherman: No luck today then, Ishmael?

INTRODUCTION

Adapting the Story

Read the story on page 71 and annotate it, using contrasting colours, to show:

PC

- Which parts of the text you will convert to lines spoken by the characters
- Which parts of the text you will convert to sound effects
- Where you will add music
- Where you will add silence
- How many scenes there will be and where scene breaks will come

Use the annotated story to plan out your script under these headings:

- Scene
- Voice/speaker
- Spoken words/script
- Sounds and music

DEVELOPMENT

Writing the Script

You are going to develop your plan for the play version of *The Daughter of the Sea* into a radio script.

Begin by reviewing the plan to ensure that you have chosen the right moments to use for speech, sound effects, music or silence. Remember every moment needs make the right impact on the listener.

Now follow the conventions of the model script below and write your script in full.

THE DAUGHTER OF THE SEA

SCENE 1

UNEARTHLY MUSIC WITH HINTS OF SEA SHANTIES

FADE UP TO SOUNDS OF SQUALLS OF WIND AND SEAGULLS CALLING

NARRATOR: Ishmael was a fisherman who had no luck. All the village fishermen returned with their nets full. All but him.

SOUND OF MALE LAUGHTER

FISHERMAN: No luck today then, Ishmael?

ISHMAEL: No Dougie, and you know it only too well.

MORE MALE LAUGHTER.

The Daughter of the Sea

Ishmael was a fisherman who had no luck. He lived on an island far to the north, in a village made rich with the wealth of the sea. All who went out in boats returned with nets full. All but him. Empty nets, every day. How they laughed, and how he cursed. A luckless man, he was, till he met the daughter of the sea. Was she a woman in a seal's skin or a seal in a woman's skin? He saw her first as a seal, as he was dragging his boat in from the shore one evening, her head above the waves, but a singing with a human voice. He hid and he watched as she came into shore, and the light from the wavetops flashed in his eyes. Now she was a woman, singing and walking nightlong on the beach.

Next night the same, and the next after. Ishmael was entranced and knew he must have her. So on the third night he lay in wait and flung his net over her. She was the best catch he had ever made. For she'd stay with him, she said, be his wife good and true. Only he was never to raise a hand against nor strike her, for if he did that he would lose her forever.

With his wife came Ishmael's luck and the wealth of the sea. Every day a full net, while others' now were empty. So he grew rich and bought their boats, and grew richer still. Now no one fished without his leave. Master of the village, master of the sea. There he was, in his grand house on the clifftop, with his fine, fair wife and their three fair children. All girls. All like their mother.

Came his birthday and he gave a feast, a grand occasion to which all were invited. Well-fed and bellies full. But when Ishmael called for silence and stood to speak, he opened his mouth and let fly a belch. There was a stony silence and noone dared to laugh - except his wife. Sitting beside him, She laughed and kept on laughing, shaming him, She wouldn't shut up, so he struck her, a flat-hand slap cracked through the room. She said nothing but rose and left. He followed after, down to the shore where she went with her children, walking with them into the sea. He plunged through the waves but the sea rose against him, a roaring wave flinging him back. A wave that rose higher and fell on the village. Boats wrecked, harbour smashed. The luck of the sea was dragged back to the deep.

The sea's calm now, the village gone, long abandoned. Deserted, except for Ishmael. See him there, an old man in rags. He stands on the shoreline, calls out to the ocean: "Come back! Come back to me." So he calls, but she never comes.

When your script is complete, rehearse it – each taking one or more parts. One of you should take on the role of director and make notes as scenes are rehearsed on how they might be improved.

Finally, tape your script so that it can be played to the class.

PLENARY

Listen as the different adaptations of *The Daughter of the Sea* are played to you.

Note down, for later discussion, any memorable moments in each performance that made real impact.

Be prepared to answer questions from the class on decisions you took in your own adaptation.

29 Advertising on TV

OBJECTIVES *TR3*, TR9, TW17, SL7

- **To recognise how texts are shaped by the technology they use, e.g. *the use of sound and image in computer animation***
- **To integrate evidence into writing to support analysis or conclusions, e.g. *data, quotations***
- **To listen for a specific purpose, paying sustained attention and selecting for comment or question that which is relevant to the agreed focus**

Extra Resources

Necessary: Starter – video tapes of two recent television advertisements which exemplify the strong link between text, sound and image.

In this lesson you will investigate how words, sounds and images are used in television advertisements to create meaning.

STARTER

Analysing Ads

You will be shown two advertisements that have recently appeared on the television. Before you watch them, draw up a grid like the one below.

As you watch, write the name of the product the advert is selling and make brief notes about each of the features below. Also indicate which feature is the most memorable.

- Storyline, setting, characters
- Dialogue
- Music/sound effects
- Catchphrase

Be prepared to share your notes with the rest of the class.

INTRODUCTION

Words, Sounds and Music

You are going to consider the conventions for making television advertisements. View the two ads again, this time choose one and answer the following questions:

- What type of language is used in the catchphrase, e.g. formal or informal?
- What makes the catchphrase memorable?
- How do the words and images work together?
- What kind of sounds are used in the ad?
- What does any dialogue used tell you about the product?

Share your notes to produce a class set of comments on the way image, sound and words work together in each of the advertisements.

INFO

Ads That Tell A Story

Story-telling ads represent a successful genre in TV advertising. Often these advertisements come in a series of three, presenting the same characters in different settings and developing their relationship. The idea is that by relating to the story the viewer is more likely to remember the product and to purchase it.

DEVELOPMENT

In-depth Analysis

Study the images from the Nescafe Gold Blend ad on page 73. Then read the captions to get a sense of the story and the sounds that are used. Then make notes on:

- Target audience
- Setting
- Characters
- The story told by the ad
- Speech/dialogue
- Info given about product
- Music used/including lyrics
- Other sound effects used
- Catchphrase

Turn your notes into a commentary on the advert's effectiveness in selling the product. Use the writing frame below to guide you.

Product name/who it is aimed at

Para 1: Brief summary of how the story of the ad unfolds. Who are the main characters? Who is telling the story?

Para 2: Explain what part the product plays in the story. Other information given about the product/or qualities of the product emphasised.

1

(ES) View along the a tent where a man is lying to the left of the shot and a woman to the right.
There are various African sculptures, masks and lights decorating the tent.
Woman: Why are we doing this?
Man switches on tape machine
Sounds of animals screeching from the tape

2

(Two shot) View over man's legs to woman's side of the tent.
Woman: This is silly.
Man: Coffee?
Woman tries to take the cup he offers
Man: No.
Woman: Ugh, now what?
Sound of lion roaring and insects chirruping

3

(MS) Looking at man
Man: Where are we?
Woman: I'm in a tent with my insane boyfriend.

4

(C/U) Woman drinking from her coffee mug
African drums play loudly with African tribal singing
V/O: Stir your senses with the fresh taste and rich aroma of Nescafe Gold Blend.
The coffee lovers' coffee.

5

(MS) Looking at woman
Woman: Okay, I'm on safari with some gorgeous bloke who made me a cup of Gold Blend in the back of his Landrover.
African drums continue

6

(C/U) Man looking lovingly
Man: A year ago.
Woman: Today?
African drums continue

7

(MS) Man raising his coffee cup
Man: Happy Anniversary.
African drums fade out

8

(LS) Tent lit up at night on top of a city town house
Clink of coffee cups from inside
Faint night-time traffic noise from street below

Para 3: Explain how sounds and music enhance the atmosphere created by the dialogue/setting

Para 4: Summarise the way the ad sells the product and why/if you feel the catchphrase is memorable.

Swap commentaries with your partner. Read each other's work and make separate notes on how it might be improved to give a fuller view of the word, sound and image elements in the advertisement.

PLENARY

As a class, decide on the three most important ingredients in making a TV advertisement successful.

30 Different Audiences

OBJECTIVES TR8, TR9, *TW3*, SL10

- **To investigate how meaning are changed when information is presented in different forms or transposed into different media.**
- **To recognise how texts are shaped by the technology they use, e.g. *the use of sound and image in computer animation***
- **To use talk to question, hypothesise, speculate, evaluate, solve problems and develop thinking about complex issues and ideas**

Extra Resources

Necessary: Introduction and Development – two taped ads from ITV1 prime time evening viewing and two ads from ITV1 mid-morning/ afternoon programming – to show men and women in different roles.

In this section you will look at what media texts tell us about our society. You'll focus on how men and women are represented in television ads at different viewing times.

STARTER

Specialist Audiences

With more and more satellite and cable channels available, there is an increasing number of **niche** channels which target people with specialist interests.

Identify the target audience for each of these specialist channels. Then brainstorm the products that each might advertise.

- Sky Sports
- The History Channel
- Discovery Channel
- Men and Motors
- Fashion TV
- Animal Planet

Be ready to share your ideas with the class.

INFO

Prime Time And Off-Peak

One of the most popular times to advertise on TV is in the evening between 6pm and 10pm. This is known as **prime time**, i.e. when a mass audience is likely to be tuned in. Advertising slots are at their most expensive during prime viewing time. Advertising is not as costly during **off-peak** viewing times, such as the mid-afternoon.

INTRODUCTION

Audiences for Different Times

You will be shown several television ads recorded from ITV1. The first two were recorded during **prime time** viewing. The next two were recorded at **off-peak** viewing time.

Draw up a grid like the one below. Then tick each row that matches the target audience for each product. Use the last two rows to record whether the product is intended for work or recreation. In this way, you will define the audience for the products advertised.

Prime time ads

Audience	Product 1	Product 2
Males		
Females		
Under12		
12–17		
18+		
Work		
Recreation		

Now make notes on the roles of both men and women in the four ads. Are there any differences in these roles between the prime time ads and the off-peak ads? What does this tell you about the qualities of their target audiences?

DEVELOPMENT

A Wide Appeal

You are going to analyse a prime time ad in some detail. It is the advertisement for Lynx Pulse deodorant shown opposite. It employs humour and interesting gender representation to persuade the viewer to buy the product.

Begin by discussing the following questions. Take notes as you go along.

- What makes the ad amusing?

Story summary:

A geeky guy in a bar launches into a disco routine as a new track comes on. His expert dancing attracts the attention of two lovely girls who join him. Lynx Pulse is only revealed as the product at the end.

- What by implication draws the girls to the man?
- What is the atmosphere created?
- How does the name/image of the product at the end link to the bar scene?
- Who will the ad appeal to?

Using your notes, prepare a group statement that explains what it is about this ad that will appeal to the prime-time audience.

PLENARY

Using your research into prime-time and off-peak audiences, discuss the best time of day to advertise these products on ITV1.

- Computer game
- Toilet cleaner
- Spanish holiday
- Cornflakes
- Car polish
- Hair colourant

31 Analysing Storyboards

OBJECTIVES TR9, TW11, SL9

- **To recognise how texts are shaped by the technology they use, e.g. *the use of sound and image in computer animation***
- **To explain complex ideas and information clearly, e.g. *defining principles, explaining a scientific process***
- **To reflect on their individual strengths as contributors to group talk and identify points and opportunities for development**

In this lesson you will analyse the image and sound content of a storyboard.

STARTER

The Power of the Image

The collection of images on page 77 is a **storyboard** advertising a familiar product.

First consider the power of the images alone. With a partner, summarise what is happening in the storyboard. Write one sentence for each frame to describe the action.

INTRODUCTION

Different Shots

An ad is like a short scripted story. It tells the story by using shots of different sizes and varying camera angles. The size of a shot is determined by how much of an image fills the **frame**, which is what we see on our screens.

Before going further, turn to pages 116-117 where the different types of shot and camera angle are explained. You will be using these terms to analyse the storyboard.

Reconsider each frame of the storyboard opposite in terms of 'size of shot' and camera angle. Be prepared to use your notes to explain what you think is the impact on the audience of the shots and camera angles used. The first frame has been done for you.

Frame 1 is a mid shot – focusing on Tony the Tiger in the foreground. It also allows the viewer to see the boy with the bowl of Frosties in the background.

DEVELOPMENT

Sound Elements

Apart from the images, how else information is conveyed by a storyboard?

Consider the types of sounds which often accompany the images in a storyboard.

- *Speech* – dialogue when two or more characters speak to each other or a voice-over when an 'off-screen' voice gives the viewer information
- *Extraneous/background sound*, e.g. cars going by, birds singing
- *Silence* – dramatic and often used for a key moment
- *Music* – either played throughout the advertisement or just at specific moments, e.g. a jingle at the end
- *Sound effects* – sounds created to match the action on the screen – particularly important in an animation

Each group should choose one of the above types of sound and explain how it is or might be used in the Frosties advertisement opposite. Make a note of your conclusions.

Now look at the captions on the storyboard. Each group will focus on just one. Think about how the words fit with the image. Write down what the caption adds that the image and sound elements could not convey alone.

Example:

Frame 1: The story caption gives us a sense of the movement in the sequence.

PLENARY

Share your notes on the visual, sound and text elements of the Frosties storyboard.

Draft a class list of the main features of a successful storyboard.

Open on a 10 year old boy, sitting in the lounge and we can see a box of Kellogg's Frosties in the background.

Suddenly, a large stripe falls from above and lands in the middle of the floor. Our boy looks at it with slight surprise but no sooner has the stripe landed than Tony the Tiger leaps onto it from above clutching a pile of Tiger stripes.

Tony: (With his usual gusto and enthusiasm) Let's go out and earn some stripes.

Boy: OK Tony, you're on.

He jumps with all his Tiger might off the back step and lands two-pawed on the garden path. He whacks a sticker on the ground to mark his distance. The boy then hurls himself out of the door. He lands, beating Tony's stripe by a few inches.

He slaps down his stripe in triumph.

Tony zooms off through the shrubs at the back of the garden. The boy races after him and finds himself in a park. There's a game of 3-a-side football going on, and straightaway Tony sets off towards one of the goals, which is marked on the side of a wall, and whacks a stripe right in the top right corner.

Meanwhile, the boy has joined in the game of football, which is clearly being played by some of his mates. We see him volley the ball towards the goal. It hits the stripe target perfectly, and he runs towards Tony in celebration. His mates realise what is going on, and they join in. Tony dashes off through some bushes eager to set the next challenge. The boys all follow.

They emerge into a small clearing in a forest. Tony and the boys jump on to quad bikes, and whiz off into the distance. Cut to see Tony doing a spectacular jump and we see a series of stripes that have been slapped on tree stumps by the side of the jump and Tony calls out the boy's score as he passes.

"Three stripes"...

Our hero boy jumps last and just manages to out-do the others.

..."Four stripes" shouts Tony, and the boy clenches his fist in triumph as he passes.

We see Tony running towards the camera, which pulls back.

***Tony**: I've put Tiger stripes in special packs of Frosties.*

The camera keeps pulling back, and we see Tony leap onto a death-slide. He hurtles towards us.

***Tony**: But make sure you earn them.*

He slaps his last sticker on the camera lens. On it we see the super: Frosties packshot, and EARN YOUR STRIPES.

© 2003 Kellogg Company

32 Creating a TV Ad

OBJECTIVES TR7, TR9, *TW3*, SL9

- To identify the ways implied and explicit meanings are conveyed in different texts, e.g. *irony, satire*
- To recognise how texts are shaped by the technology they use, e.g. *the use of sound and image in a computer animation*
- To reflect on their individual strengths as contributors to group talk and identify points and opportunities for development

In this section you will learn how to use a combination of words and images in order to persuade people to buy a product.

STARTER

Words that Sell

Here are some adjectives that are used in television advertisements. For each one, say what kind of product it might describe.

Then think of another word that could have been used in its place. Use a thesaurus to help you.

- Smooth
- Fragrance
- Sleek
- Convenient
- Tasty
- Masculine

Share your ideas and come up with a class list of alternative adjectives for each word.

INFO

Product Brief

A product brief is the information about a new product supplied by the maker to the advertising agency. From this information an advertising campaign will be shaped.

INTRODUCTION

Planning your Storyboard

Read the **product brief** for the new chocolate bar, Chocochoc, on page 79.

Note down what these details tell you about:

- The content of the product and its name
- The target audience
- What its USPs are
- The kind of image the makers would like the bar to have

You are going to devise the storyboard for the 20 second TV advertisement that will launch this product. Begin by brainstorming ideas for the story behind the ad. Use your notes to prompt storylines that might be right for Chocochoc.

Agree which storyline you are going to use and start to map it out in terms of the five stages of narrative:

Introduction
↓
Development
↓
Complication
↓
Crisis
↓
Resolution

Make firm decisions about the characters and setting for your ad. Decide how many frames your storyboard will have and discuss the images that might go with each stage of the story. (Aim for no more than 8 frames.)

Consider carefully the type of shots you will use, e.g. close up or long shot. To review the types of camera shots and angles available, turn to page 116 where these are explained.

Draw out your draft storyboard and sketch in the images. Leave plenty of room for the sound text and speech text that will be added next.

DEVELOPMENT

Adding Sound, Speech and Text

Now that you have the visual content of your storyboard in place, look back at pages 76-77 where the types of sound and speech content in storyboards are considered.

Discuss who will deliver the speech content in your advertisement:

- Will it be through both characters and a voice-over?
- Will it be just through a voice-over?

Product brief: Chocochoc

Target Audience
Main audience:
Men and women – aged 10-18 years
Secondary audience:
Older women – 20 +

Qualities
Smooth
Too much chocolate!
Sleek
Slim – pocket/handbag sized
'Extra' flavour

Shape
A slim 'finger' of chocolate

Packaging
Bar itself wrapped in gold foil (luxury)
Outer paper wrapping is patterned with gold and white diagonal stripes (very plush/chic).
The name 'Chocochoc' appears horizontally on a gold panel running almost the length of the bar.

Price and weight
50 pence
49 grammes

- Will the speech give any key information about the product?

Decide what text will appear in the ad:

- Will you just feature a slogan at the end?
- Will you include text by other means – e.g. signs within images?
- Will you include emotive words to 'sell' the product?

Think about the sound effects and music your story will require.

Now write the text, speech and sound captions for your board. Once these are in place you may need to make adjustments to your image content so that all four elements work together.

Be ready to discuss your storyboard in class.

PLENARY

Swap advertisement storyboards with another group. Consider their idea for an advertisement.

- How does it bring image, sound, text and speech together?
- Which elements work particularly well?
- Do you think it will make a persuasive ad? Explain your reasons.

Offer your feedback to the class.

33 Analysing Pre-school comics

OBJECTIVES TR8, TW4, TW9

- **To analyse how media texts influence and are influenced by readers, e.g. *interactive programmes, selection of news items***
- **To choose, use and evaluate a range of presentational devices, on paper and on screen**
- **To integrate diverse information into a coherent and comprehensive account**

Extra Resources

Optional: Introduction – examples of books, computer games and comics for pre-school children.

In this lesson you will look at how words and pictures are used in different media products to encourage young children to read.

STARTER

Toddler Tastes

With a partner, think about the types of media products you used to enjoy before you went to school. If you know any young children, think about what print or moving image media they like best. Then in a grid like the one below give examples of products that are particular favourites with this age group.

Product	Example	Main appeal
Television		
Books		
Comics		
Cinema		
Music CDs		
Computer games		

Be ready to share your ideas with the class and to discuss how media products for this audience have changed since you were a toddler.

INTRODUCTION

Attracting the Audience

Many of these media products present stories. Think about what the stories in these products have in common. Consider the following and make notes to show how these features make them appealing to the pre-school audience.

- Content
  Characters: what types of character are featured? For example, are they male or female, from different ethnic groups, young or old? Are they puppets, models or cartoons? What qualities do the characters have? An example has been modelled below.
  The story: how does the plot develop? What settings are used?
- Visual style
  How are pictures used to convey meaning? How are typography and graphics used to make the product attractive?

Example:

Content

Characters: in 'Teletubbies' for example there are five main characters – Tinky Winky and Dipsy are boys and Lala and Po are girls. Dipsy might represent a different ethnic group. Noo Noo has qualities both of a pet and a domestic robot.

The characters in the 'Jellikins' story opposite are two bears, one light who is called Strum and one dark who is called Bouncey. They appear to be male and are dressed in typical pirate costumes. This will appeal to pre-school children's love of dressing up.

reading

Shipwrecked

DEVELOPMENT

Focusing on the Frames

In writing for a pre-school audience, pictures are a crucial part of telling the story. They encourage the audience, who probably cannot read, to try and understand what the words mean.

Building on your notes from the Introduction, answer the following questions. Note down in your grid what you see in each frame of the *Shipwrecked* story on page 81 from the comic *Jellikins*.

	1st Frame	2nd Fr
What is happening?		
Who are the characters?		
What are they wearing?		
Where are they?		
What objects are they using?		
What else can you see?		

The action in each of these **frames** is seen from a slightly different angle or **point-of-view**. Continuing in your pairs, discuss what the reader is encouraged to focus on in each frame.

Write down the difference each point-of-view makes to what the frame conveys. For example:

Frame 1 uses an establishing shot to show the two main characters and the setting for the story. The focus is clearly on the two bears.

(For more on point-of-view and the types of shot that can be used in a print or moving image story, see pages 116-119.)

Now consider the style of the print elements in the *Jellikins* story. Note down how the style and language of the following appeal to the pre-school audience and help them 'read' the story. Include comments about:

- Story title
- Style of the typography
- Caption-like text in boxes
- Simple rhyming text
- Use of circled numbers

The example below will guide you.

The title is quite large compared to the captions and follows the shape of a wave to signify visually to the reader that the story is set at sea (in this case a jelly sea). The sans serif font is large, well spaced and simple so that the young reader can identify letters, combinations of letters, whole words and a sentence. There are 4 or 5 words per line and every caption has the second and fourth line rhyming; young children learn to read and write through repetition and rhyme.

Using your notes, write an analytical commentary of how the printed and visual features of the *Jellikins* page encourage a pre-school audience to engage with and understand the story.

The following writing frame should help you to structure your ideas.

Analysis of the 'Jellikins' story

Visual elements

Para 1: Outline the narrative sequence used in the 'Jellikins' story. Comment when and if it is different from this order:

* Introduction - establish setting/characters/plot
* Development
* Complication
* Crisis
* Resolution

Explain how the storyline would keep the interest of readers under five.

Para 2: Examine the style of the images, the colours used and objects included. Explain how these would appeal to the audience.

Print elements

Para 3 Analyse each type of print used and remember to describe it and then EXPLAIN how it creates meaning for the pre-school audience.

* Title and story text styles
* Caption-like text
* Speech
* Numbered illustrations

Conclusion

Draw together your ideas on the print and visual elements of the story and how they are juxtaposed to create maximum impact on an under-fives audience.

PLENARY

Listen as one commentary on the *Jellikins* story is read to the class.

Remember the analysis should show how the **juxtaposition** of visuals and printed text work together to communicate an entertaining and educational narrative to a very young audience.

Give positive feedback, and add any points that the commentary has not mentioned.

34 Bob the Story Builder

OBJECTIVES TR8 TW4 SL4

- **To analyse how media texts influence and are influenced by readers, e.g. *interactive programmes, selection of news items***
- **To choose, use and evaluate a range of presentational devices, on paper and on screen**
- **To reflect and evaluate your own skills, strategies and successes as listeners in a variety of contexts**

In this section you will explore a typical media writing job: to take somebody else's characters and provide a comic book story for them.

STARTER

Matching Characters to Plots

Write down the names of the *Bob the Builder* characters pictured on the CBeebies webpage opposite. For each name write a couple of sentences on what you think it tells us about the character it belongs to.

Now choose six characters and think up a *Bob the Builder* storyline that each one might star in. Briefly explain your reasons in a few sentences.

INTRODUCTION

Creating a Story Plan

Script writers are often asked to write one of a series of scripts about the same set of characters. Your task will be similar: to produce a comic book story with the 'cast' of *Bob the Builder*. Begin by choosing:

- Three characters, including Bob or Wendy
- A special place for the story setting, e.g. a park
- The machines which will play the most important part

Draft out the text for seven of the eight frames in your story but do not write the ending. Remember to use the language features of writing for pre-school children:

- Simple dialogue
- Use of past tense
- Punctuation - especially exclamation mark/ question mark
- Simple vocabulary/spelling

Remember also that the themes and actions of the characters should be suitable for a pre-school audience.

The model story plan below will guide you.

1 One bright windy day, Wendy was looking for Bob.
'Now where is Bob?' asked Wendy.

2 Bob was busy fixing a fence that had blown over when Wendy found him.
'Bob, Mrs Green has got a problem at the corner shop. Her sign needs fixing.'
'I'm on my way,' said Bob.

3 Bob soon arrived with Lofty and his tools.
Mrs Green was worried the sign was going to fall off.

4 Lofty lifted Bob up to fix the sign.
Just then a huge gust of wind blew the sign to the ground.
'Oh no!' said Bob.

Now swap story plans with a partner. Consider the story carefully and then write the ending in the form of the text for the final frame.

DEVELOPMENT

Constructing the Visuals

Take your story plan forward by beginning to sketch ideas for the images that will accompany the text for each frame.

Consider:

- The main event that will make the most visual impact on a young reader
- The point-of-view for each frame
- The focus on key characters

(For more on point-of-view and the types of shot that can be used in a print or moving image story, see pages 116-119. Also use your analysis of the *Jellikins* story to guide you.)

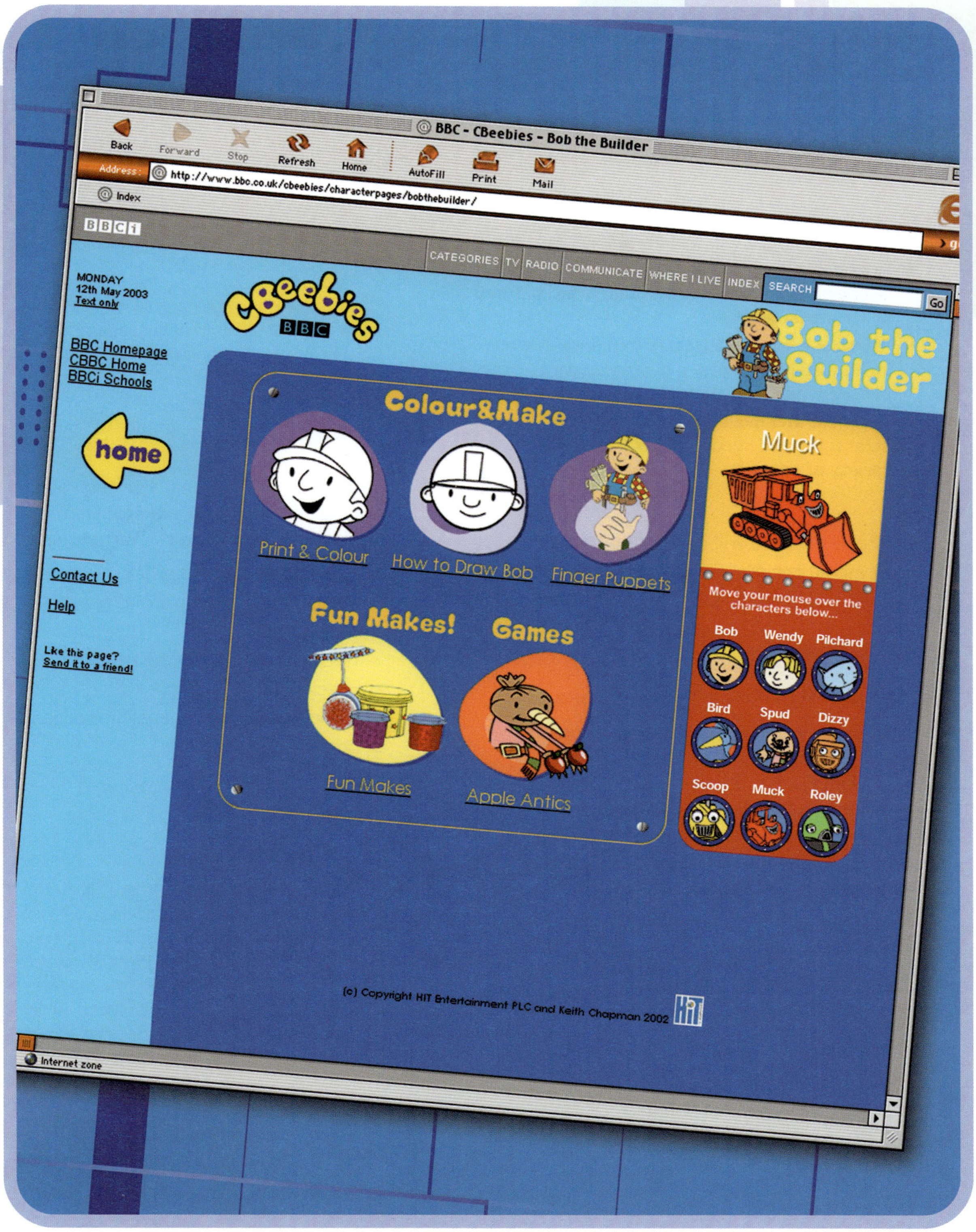

Produce a final version of your story either on paper or on screen.

Concentrate on refining your text to match the images and to increase appeal to the pre-school audience.

PLENARY

Listen as several of the *Bob the Builder* stories are presented to the class.

As you listen, identify the print and visual features which the writers have included to guarantee children under five will enjoy their stories.

Feed back your comments to the class.

35 Pleasing Older Audiences

OBJECTIVES TR4, TR8, SL4

- **To evaluate the relevance, reliability and validity of information available through print, ICT and other media sources**
- **To analyse how media texts influence and are influenced by readers, e.g. *interactive programmes, selection of news items***
- **To reflect and evaluate your own skills, strategies and successes as listeners in a variety of contexts**

Extra Resources

Optional: Plenary - a copy of the most recent *My Weekly* to help students judge how well their articles matched the magazine's audience.

In this lesson you will learn about writing in print media for audiences comprising of retired and older people.

STARTER

Targeting Older Audiences

With a partner, read the list of programme genres and titles below. Match each programme (A-I) to its genre (1-9). Write your answers as a list. Then note down next to each item whether the programme will appeal to an older audience or a younger audience. Some may appeal to both.

Titles	Genres
A Panorama	1 Soaps
B Big Brother	2 Documentaries
C Top of the Pops	3 Historical
D The Weakest Link	4 Dramas
E A Touch of Frost	5 Music shows
F Time Team	6 Reality TV
G My Family	7 Current affairs
H 6 o'clock news	8 Game shows
I Coronation Street	9 Sit com

Discuss as a class if you are surprised by the amount of overlap between the lists of viewing preferences for older and young audiences.

INTRODUCTION

Analysing the Cover

Working in small groups, look at the cover of *My Weekly* shown opposite and read the panel of info on its readership. For each element in the list below, give an example from the cover and its main appeal to the target audience.

- Typography and size of title
- Main image (photographic/graphic/drawing)
- Use of colour
- Teaser lines to draw the reader in
- Special offers
- Layout (how print/images are organised)
- Cost

INFO

Readership Profile

My Weekly has a readership of around 820,000 of which 92% is female. 19% of readers are aged between 55 and 64 and 47% fall into the 65+ bracket. *My Weekly* readers are active women with interests in gardening, eating out and shopping. Older readers are part of the grey market which is growing in both size and economic importance.

DEVELOPMENT

Articles to Suit the Audience

Read the contents page from *My Weekly* shown opposite. Now devise three articles that you think would appeal to the readers of the magazine. For each article write:

- A short outline of what the article is about
- A headline for the article
- An idea for a photograph or illustration to accompany the article

Follow the model for an article on page 87.

<u>Outline</u>: Makeover article. Story of an older lady who has found romance on holiday and now plans to marry. She will be given new ideas for makeup, hair and clothes just before the wedding.

<u>Headline</u>: 'Just one look...' [leading into first para 'was all it took... when Jane met Ian...']

<u>Photographs</u>: Jane before her makeover; 2 images of Jane having her hair and makeup done; 4 images of Jane in her new clothes – captions to give prices and retailers' details.

Now write the introductory paragraph for one of your articles.

PLENARY

One pair will present their outline for three articles for *My Weekly* and read the first paragraph of their chosen article.

Feed back your comments on how successful their ideas would be for an older audience and why.

Review together how a piece of journalism for an older audience differs from another. You could compare your articles with those in the latest issue of *My Weekly*.

36 Programming for Older People

OBJECTIVES TR4, TR8, TW1

- **To evaluate the relevance, reliability and validity of information available through print, ICT and other media sources**
- **To analyse how media texts influence and are influenced by readers, e.g. *interactive programmes, selection of news items***
- **To review their ability to write for a range of purposes and audiences, recognising strengths and weaknesses and identifying skills for further development**

In this lesson you will look at examples of how television and radio target older and retired people. You will also design a programme of your own aimed at this audience.

STARTER

Stereotyping through Names

Below is a list of names that are used to describe older people. What do you notice about the names? Try to match each of these names to one of the pictures below.

- Old codger
- Grandad
- Granny
- OAP
- Senior Citizen
- Old lady
- Old boy
- Gramps
- Old timer

Were you uncomfortable using any of the labels? Were they examples of negative stereotyping? Which name would you prefer to be given when you are older?

INFO

Stereotyping

Certain 'types' of people are represented in the media in typical or stereotypical ways such as the 'dumb blonde' or 'deaf pensioner'. This leads to the audience attaching positive or negative values to not just the individuals depicted but to all people of that 'type'. Negative stereotyping concerning race, gender, class, religion, disability or sexual orientation can result in unfair or abusive treatment of certain groups.

INTRODUCTION

Programme Selections

Using the listings magazines on page 89 identify any television or radio programme that you think is aimed at older or retired people. Note down what it is about and why it will appeal to this audience in a grid like this:

Programme	Content	Appeal

INFO

The Grey Market

By 2011 there will be 12 million pensioners in Britain. People aged over 65 will then outnumber children aged under 16. This growing grey market has time and money available. Between 1995 and 2001 pensioners' incomes rose by around 17% whilst average earnings rose 9%. However, it is estimated that 21% of pensioners cannot meet their monthly bills.

DEVELOPMENT

Planning your Programme

Imagine you have been asked to create a half-hour travel programme aimed at people aged over 55. Remember that many older people are highly active.

- What will be the title of your programme?
- When do you think would be the best time to broadcast it and on which channel?
- Write a short plan for your programme. You will need to explain what would be in the programme and give details, for example, about who might present it. Use the example below as a guide on what to include.

Example:

TV company: Channel 4 timing 1.25 pm before the afternoon film

Genre: travelogue/video diary

Presenter: Prunella Scales (Granny character in the Tesco's ads)

Destination: Mongolia

* *Starts in Mongolian desert*
* *Cuts back to North London at home*
* *Returns to adventure in desert - video diary/surviving on horseback with Mongolian riders/living in Yurts/diet etc.../warts and all*
* *Comic cuts, e.g. flashback to 'ordinary life' in London/family/buses*
* *Conclusion: pros/cons - rating/(especially for older travellers)*

PLENARY

Look back at your ideas for a programme. If you were to devise a trailer for it, what would be its **unique selling point**? How would you emphasise this in order to get an older audience hooked?

37 Analysing TV Trailers

OBJECTIVES W7, *TR3*, TR4, TR8,

- **To recognise layers of meaning in the writer's choice of words, e.g. *connotation, implied meaning, different types or multiple meanings***
- **To evaluate the relevance, reliability and validity of information available through print, ICT and other media sources**
- **To analyse how media texts influence and are influenced by readers, e.g. *interactive programmes, selection of news items***

Extra Resources

Optional: Development – a recent trailer screened on TV for a new TV series.

In this lesson you will explore the conventions of TV trailers and consider how they are used to hook viewers and so promote the product.

STARTER

Hooking the Viewer

TV trailers are sometimes referred to as a 'tease' – something that will motivate people to watch it for the first time or to watch the next episode.

One way in which trailers 'hook' viewers into watching the programme is through the language of the voice-over. Discuss each of the following voice-over hooks to bring out the meaning behind the persuasive phrasing.

- If you think you were scared before...
- Never seen before: Bruce Willis as the baby-faced killer double-crossed by Keanu Reeves
- From the makers of... comes...
- Winner of 3 BAFTAs...
- Coming to BBC1 a new series using ground-breaking technology...

INTRODUCTION

What Makes a Good Trailer?

Using the following list, analyse your current favourite TV trailer. Decide how it uses these elements to reach its audience.

- Emphasis on the genre of programme
- Editing: rapid cuts for pace
- Names of the stars/actors who appear in it
- Enticing details about the story in the voice-over/clips from dialogue
- Music
- Sound effects

INFO

Timing Trailers

It is important that a TV programme trailer goes out during programming aimed at a similar audience. For example, *Samurai Jack* is an animated series on the CNX channel. Its trailer is aired in the 3.00-6.00 p.m. children's slot. The programme is screened at 6 p.m. at the end of this slot in the schedules. The main audience is boys aged 10-15 but extends to 16-25 year-old men.

DEVELOPMENT

Writing an Analysis

Look carefully at the still images and captions from the trailer for *Samurai Jack* on page 91. (If you prefer you could use a taped trailer of your choosing.)

The central character is a Samurai warrior who travels back through time facing moral dilemmas and combating evil. The images and music are influenced by Japanese culture.

Working with a partner, note down answers to the following questions:

- What type or genre of programme is the trailer advertising?
- What does the voice-over tell you?
- Who are the main character(s) featured in the trailer? What do you learn about them?
- What situations or parts of the story (narrative) does the trailer focus on? Why?
- What parts of the trailer would make the target audience want to watch the series?

Write an analysis of the trailer drawing upon your notes and the writing frame on page 91.

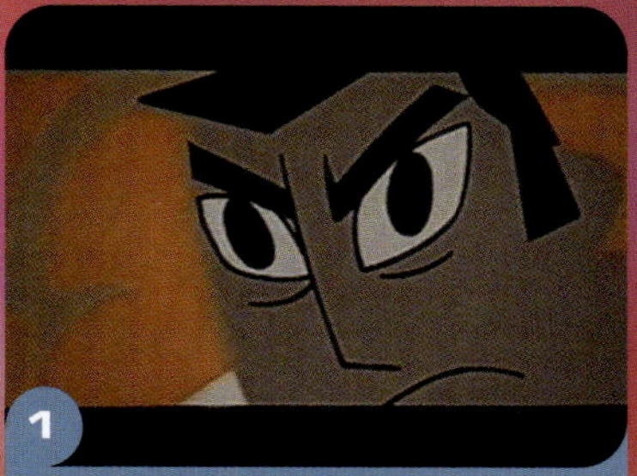

1

Samurai Jack's father's voice: 'Always be alert my son.'
Sound effect: Samurai sword being drawn.

2

V/O: In the future
Text on screen: IN THE FUTURE
Sound effect: Japanese drums

3

V/O: Evil
Text on screen: EVIL
Music: Fast club dance music

4

V/O: Takes many forms
Text on screen: TAKES MANY FORMS
Music: Fast club dance music continues

5

Music: Fast club dance music continues

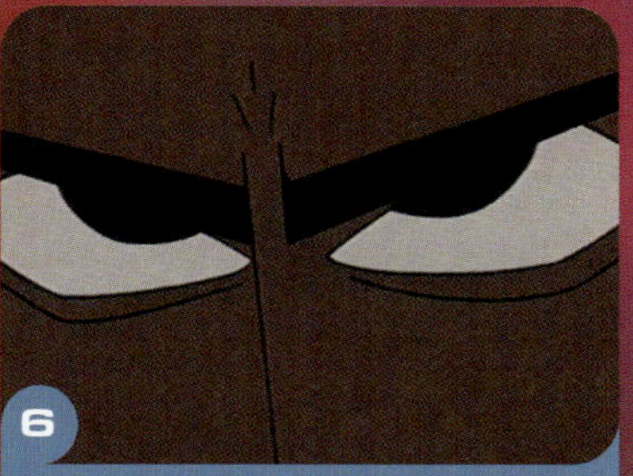

6

V/O: And our only hope is one man
Text on screen: OUR ONLY HOPE IS ONE MAN
Music: Fast club dance music continues

7

V/O: From the past
Text on screen: FROM THE PAST
Music: Fast club dance music continues

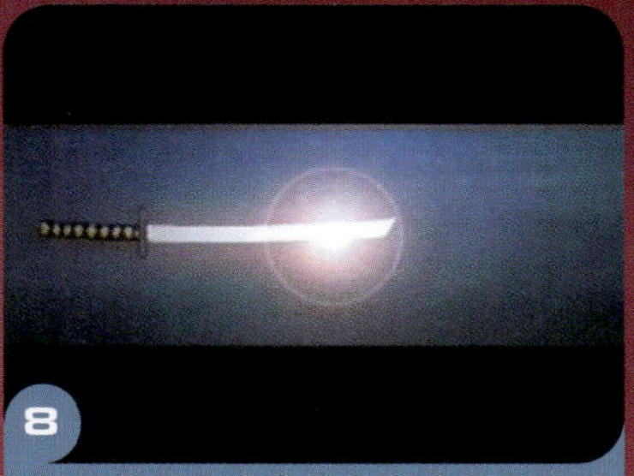

8

Samurai Jack: 'I will not fail you, father.'
Music: Fast club dance music fades slightly

9

V/O: Follow the legend. New episodes of Samurai Jack next Friday at 5.30 on Cartoon Network.
Music: Dance music ends dramatically
Sound effect: Right at the end - an oriental-sounding bell

Intro: facts concerning the product - those highlighted in voice-over

Para 1: analysis of genre conventions: character and plot

Para 2: analysis of narrative sequence of trailer, i.e. how it is organised

Para 3: how the trailer appeals to both new and existing viewers

Conclusion: assess how successful the trailer is in persuading its target audience to watch the series - fresh viewers and existing viewers

PLENARY

Use your analysis to give an explanation to the class of how the *Samurai Jack* trailer works.

Give your view on how successfully the images, spoken elements and sounds combine to convince its audience to watch.

38 Devising a TV Trailer

OBJECTIVES TR8, TW12, SL10

- **To analyse how media texts influence and are influenced by readers, e.g. *interactive programmes, selection of news items***
- **To exploit the potential of presentational devices when presenting information on paper or on screen, e.g. *font size, text layout, bullet points, italics***
- **To contribute to the organisation of group activity in ways that help to structure plans, solve problems and evaluate alternatives**

Extra Resources

Optional: Starter - screening of an episode from another TV drama on which students might base their own trailers.

In this lesson you have the opportunity to devise a TV trailer of your own.

STARTER

Selecting Key Scenes

Look carefully at the stills taken from an episode of the TV drama, *Down to Earth*. These together with the summary for the plot of this episode are the raw materials for the trailer you are going to devise.

(You could base your trailer on an episode from a TV drama you have watched in class.)

Begin by carefully selecting the three scenes that you are going to include. Remember they should not give the whole story away, but provide enough information to entice the viewer to watch. Each scene should fulfil a number of different purposes in conveying the following aspects of the programme:

- the characters/stars
- the setting
- the storyline (key dramatic moments)
- the genre of the programme

Now that you have selected the three scenes for your trailer, write a brief explanation of your choices. How will they draw in new viewers for the series and persuade existing viewers to watch this episode?

INTRODUCTION

Scripting the Voice-over

Using the three stills you have selected and the plot summary opposite, make notes for the voice-over script for each scene. The narrator's job is to make the programme sound exciting and interesting to the target audience, for example by reminding the audience of the actors' names or by giving some plot detail.

Refer back to the examples of language used in voice-over hooks on page 90. Incorporate some of these in your draft voice-over script.

Example:

V/O: Watch Sunday's Down to Earth when Matt gets a shock...

DEVELOPMENT

Developing your Storyboard

Now draw out a storyboard for your trailer following these stages:

- Sketch three frames to show each scene you have chosen. Decide what type of shot you will use in each frame. Make a note of this below each sketch, e.g. two shot: Frankie and Matt.
- Under each sketch write the voice-over text that you drafted in the Introduction.
- Invent snippets of dialogue from the episode that will be featured, e.g. Frankie: 'Matt, I've got news for you. You're going be a father again.'
- Include a note of any sound effects that might be needed, e.g. a sow grunting, or any music that is to be featured, e.g. clip from theme music.

Remember it is your job to make the episode appeal to the audience so they will view it.

Before going further, turn to page116 where the different types of shot and camera angle are explained.

PLENARY

Listen as groups present their TV trailer storyboards to the class.

Discuss how well they have used story content, camera angles, voice-over, dialogue and other sound elements to attract the audience.

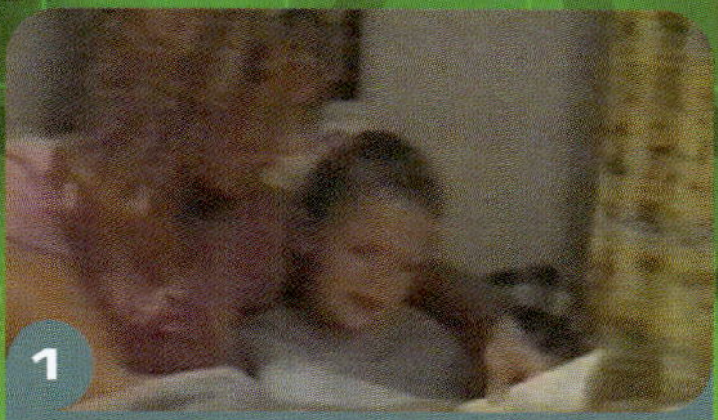

1 Frankie reads to Lucy

2 Lucy remembers her holiday with her mum in Ilfracombe

3 Frankie takes the pig pregnancy test

4 Matt gets lost on his delivery round

5 Lucy runs away to Ilfracombe

6 Lucy on the coach journey

7 Becki and Val on their way to the pop concert

8 Frankie worries where Lucy is

9 Frankie and Matt find Lucy on Lundy

Plot summary for the episode

Frankie, Matt, Becki and Lucy have just moved to Silverdale in Devon from London to run a smallholding. They will grow and market vegetables to the local community. Becki and Lucy are Matt's children by his first wife who has died. Now Matt is with Frankie.

In this episode, Lucy is not happy in her new home and decides to run away. She plans to return to Ilfracombe where she once had a holiday with her mum. Meanwhile, Matt gets lost on his first vegetable box delivery run and Frankie is helping the vet to do a pregnancy test on their sow.

The older daughter Becki persuades the vicar's daughter, Val, to go to a pop concert when they should be at a design lesson at school. When they get to the concert they get drawn into a pop video rehearsal. Becki is leading Val into trouble.

Matt comes back to help look for Lucy. Eventually, Frankie finds her on Lundy Island. She had taken the boat there from Ilfracombe to watch the puffins.

Frankie ends the episode by telling Matt he is going to be a Dad again – their pig is pregnant after all.

39 Celebrity Stories

OBJECTIVES TR4, TR8, TW16

- To evaluate the relevance, reliability and validity of information available through print, ICT and other media sources
- To analyse how media texts influence and are influenced by readers, e.g. *interactive programmes, selection of news items*
- To present a balanced view of a situation, text, issue or set of ideas, taking into account a range of evidence and opinions

In this section you will look at the ways in which elements of the mass media are interdependent. The media thus provides itself with ready-made material.

INFO

Defining The News

Newspapers have a clear function which is described by their name: they are places to find a commodity called 'news'. **News** is usually defined as those things which are new events in the world about which the general public have a need or right to know.

STARTER

Celebrity News

Read the *Madonna in Miniature* story on page 95, taken from the *Daily Mail* newspaper. It is written without any direct input from the celebrity herself. Brainstorm answers to the following questions:

- What type of news is this?
- What is the angle of the story?
- What type of text is included in the article? Is it for entertainment/information?

Conduct a ten-minute debate on whether the *Madonna in Miniature* article is **newsworthy**. One person should argue 'for' and one 'against' for two minutes.

Then questions can be taken from the 'floor'. Take a class vote to end the debate.

INTRODUCTION

Writing about Celebrities

Take a close look at the first six paragraphs of the *Madonna in miniature* story. Consider the following techniques used to convey the information about Lourdes and her likeness to her mother:

- Use of humour
- Links to photos included in the article
- Anecdotal evidence
- Direct quotation from a 'witness'

Example:

Para 1: uses a Madonna song title to give a clue to the identity of the girl in the photo.

Review the debate from the Starter. Have you changed your view on the newsworthiness of the article?

Now look carefully at the rest of the article jumbled up on the page opposite. Take the paragraphs labelled from A-H and order them as you think they appeared in the article.

Next to each letter explain the main point in the **topic sentence**.

Example:

Para 1: uses a reference to a Madonna song to attract the reader's interest.

Finally, turn to page 128 to see if your order matches that of the original article. What are the similarities and differences?

How Lourdes is like her mother (in more than just looks)

Madonna in miniature

By **Mark Reynolds**
Showbusiness Reporter

ONE of her mother's hit singles was called Who's That Girl?

Which is a question no one who saw the young lady in the sweatshirt and shorts on the right would have had to ask.

With her dark hair and bright eyes, little Lourdes is the double of her mother Madonna when she was a child.

And it is not only the superstar's looks that she has inherited. At the age of only six, Lourdes is also clearly a born entertainer.

On an after-school trip with her nanny to a sandwich bar near the family's Los Angeles home, the youngster put on an impromptu ballet display which delighted fellow shoppers.

One impressed onlooker said: 'She seemed a natural performer like her mother and appeared to have a certain amount of talent too.'

A Madonna, 44, and Ritchie moved with both her children shortly before Christmas.

B While the children enjoyed themselves, Madonna and Ritchie were busy working, with the singer filming her latest music video.

C Lourdes - Madonna's daughter by former love Carlos Leon - obviously enjoyed performing, while her half-brother Rocco entertained himself with some toy cars.

D And while her agent maintains that she and Ritchie will return to Britain 'within the next few months', the move has fuelled speculation that they may be planning a longer stay in the U.S.

E The toddler is the image of his film director father, whose movies include *Snatch* and *Lock, Stock and Two Smoking Barrels*.

F Previously, Madonna has spoken of her affection for her adopted country. 'I consider myself an English chap,' she said last year. 'I feel like I am a bit of an Anglophile because Guy is and that's what happens when you fall in love with somebody.'.

G Rocco is Madonna's two-year-old son by her British husband Guy Ritchie, and he too is clearly a chip off the old block.

H The family have left their homes in wintry England - a London house and an £8million estate in Wiltshire - for a new life in sun-drenched California.

DEVELOPMENT

Celebrity-led Stories

In contrast to the *Madonna in miniature* article, celebrity stories are also offered as features in magazines. Like the Sophie Ellis Bextor feature on this page, they might include direct information via an interview with a celebrity or reference to their earlier work.

Read the Sophie Ellis Bextor feature and make a note of examples of the following conventions:

- Frequent use of the celebrity's first name
- Informal style
- Confessional tone
- Humour
- Non-Standard English phrases
- Unfinished sentences using ellipses (...)
- Rhetorical questions

Use this example as a guide:

Non-Standard English: includes phrases like 'wonky' and 'kinda like'

Using your evidence from both the Madonna and the Sophie Ellis Bextor texts, write a comparative response.

The writing frame below will help you.

Intro: main points on representation of celebrity in each article

Para 1: Images - reliance on image/how images are used

Para 2: Language and structure - use of anecdote v use of direct info from celebrity

- use of flexible structure v use of interview-like structure

Para 3: Layout - use of unconventional v conventional techniques

Conclusion: reflect on the relationship between text, audience and purpose in both articles

News & stuff

EXCLUSIVE!

Sophie's secret writing past

She was a journalist for her school paper

She's the poshest pop star on the block these days, but when she was at school, all Sophie Ellis Bextor wanted to be was a journalist. During her time in sixth-form college, Soph was a reporter for her school magazine and *loved* writing about her favourite thing – make-up. Reading the piece – imaginatively titled, *Why I Love It: Make-up* – it's obvious that Sophie's penchant for products and experimenting with dramatic colours isn't something that started after she appeared on *Top Of The Pops*. No wonder she called her album *Read My Lips* …

Sophie on … her essentials: "My favourite is lipstick, reddy-brown preferably, but I have a soft spot for all make-up really. Obviously, concealer is an essential (unfortunately), and powder's a must for oily days."

Sophie on … eye make-up: "OK. I admit it. My eyeliner is often wonky and I never could master the liquid stuff. It usually ends up accentuating the bags under my eyes. (Yes mum, I am getting enough sleep …)"

Sophie on … trial and error: "I've made a few mistakes. Orange concealer rings a bell. But I love the thrill of experimentation. In fact, many times, I'd say getting my face ready for a night out is better than the event itself."

Sophie on … shopping for cosmetics: "The feeling I get when I walk into Boots' make-up section is similar to the exhilaration I felt when I was younger and a flash of neon pink was a signpost to Barbie territory. My pace quickens, my eyes flash and I reach to try the new mascara and lipstick."

Sophie on … her looks: "Why, I ask myself, is it so exciting to transform myself? It can't be that I feel I'll turn into Cindy Crawford – no need to break it to me gently, I've long since disillusioned myself on that one, but I think the answer lies on a similar line. I can become something else. It's kinda like Clark Kent becoming Superman. Or secretary to Catwoman. Erica to Bananaman. Err … yeah, I think I've made my point."

PLENARY

Listen as one comparative response is read to the class.

How clearly does the writing use evidence and opinion from the articles to show the differences in the two texts?

40 TV Listings Features

OBJECTIVES TR4, TR8, TW7

- To evaluate the relevance, reliability and validity of information available through print, ICT and other media sources
- To analyse how media texts influence and are influenced by readers, e.g. *interactive programmes, selection of news items*
- To explore how non-fiction texts can convey information in amusing or entertaining ways

Extra Resources

Optional: Development – a list of up-coming series gleaned from a TV guide.

In this section you will look at one type of feature writing in TV listings.

INFO

Feature Writing

Feature writing is where a journalist gets the chance to write a more in-depth article that does not rely on newsworthiness for its appeal. In TV magazines the purpose is often to promote a programme or a personality.

STARTER

Information at a Glance

New television programmes are marketed in a variety of ways: on billboards, through trailers or magazine and press advertising. In the week of their launch, pieces called features, are written in specialist TV listings magazines such as *The Radio Times* or *What's on TV*.

With a partner, read the item about *Jonathan Creek* from *What's on TV* on page 99. List four types of information offered and examples of words and phrases that inform the reader about the new series. For example:

Type of information	Example
Who's in Jonathan Creek	'Alan Davies is back. By his side again'

Discuss whether the information offered would persuade you to watch the programme. Does the feature leave any questions unanswered?

Be ready to feed back your analysis and your ideas to the class.

INTRODUCTION

What Persuades and Informs?

Read the feature on page 99 for the series, *It Shouldn't Happen on a TV Makeover Show*. List the language conventions that inform and persuade the reader and give examples. Follow the model below.

Language that informs	Language that persuades
Use of 2nd person 'You', e.g. 'You'll finally get to hear...'	Rhetorical questions, e.g. 'Ever watched...?'

Share your ideas and create a class list of conventions for TV listing features.

DEVELOPMENT

Writing a Feature

Working on your own, write a feature article for a programme of your choice. Remember your task is to:

- Gain the attention and interest of the audience by offering small pieces of enticing information about the series.
- Write persuasively
- Keep your feature between 100-120 words.

Use the class list to remind you of the conventions to build into your feature.
The model feature on page 99 should also guide you.

THE BEST OF what's on THIS WEEK

New

What have you done?

It Shouldn't Happen on a TV Makeover Show, ITV1, Sat

Ever watched a TV makeover and thought you'd be horrified if it was your home and it all went wrong? That's exactly what happened to the people in this week's *It Shouldn't Happen on a TV Makeover Show.* You'll finally get to hear the true opinions of people who have found a room that has been transformed into their idea of hell, like Sarah and Daniel Johnson, whose four children transformed their kitchen into a burger bar on a kids' makeover show. Also watch out for the usually amiable garden expert Alan Titchmarsh throwing an almighty tantrum, and builder Tommy Walsh threatening to nail Alan's feet to the floor! Meanwhile, stars including Carol Smillie and Charlie Dimmock also tell us what it's like performing a TV transformation against the clock.

Magic Man

Jonathan Creek, BBC1 Sat

Alan Davies is back as the self-effacing magician in the fourth series of *Jonathan Creek*. By his side again is Carla Borrego (Julia Sawalha) – the prim but pushy amateur detective who tries to help Jonathan solve more gripping mysteries.

In this week's first episode, the pair try to unravel the case of a policewoman who's been strangle to death in an empty gymnasium. Look out for *The Young Ones'* Adrian Edmondson who also joins the cast.

New

NEW

Stars before their Eyes?

Oblivious: Popstars, ITV1, Tues

Would you like to be on a TV gameshow and not realise it? That's the position in which both popstars and ordinary members of the public find themselves in this new series. With hidden cameras and fake TV reporters to trip them up, they are bound to be caught out time and again. Watch as the Sugababes...

PLENARY

Exchange your TV feature with a partner and review how well they have used the following:

- Snippets of information
- Persuasive language

41 Access all Areas

OBJECTIVES TR8, TW10, SL10

- To analyse how media texts influence and are influenced by readers, e.g. *interactive programmes, selection of news items*
- To explain the precise connections between ideas with clarity and an appropriate degree of formality
- To contribute to the organisation of a group activity in ways that help to structure plans, solve problems and evaluate alternatives

Extra Resources

Optional: Introduction – a taped pop/rockumentary for analysis task.

In this section you will consider the characteristics and content of the popumentary/rockumentary film genre.

INFO

Media Hybrids

The words popumentary/rockumentary describe a media product which fuses two existing genres. This is called a **hybrid**. From music we have the genres of rock and pop and from film and television we have the genre of documentary. These films document the working life of a pop/rock band through a collection of live performances integrated with interviews and 'exclusive' back-stage footage. They are also an extra promotional tool.

STARTER

The Making of a Hybrid

Before you analyse the elements of a pop/rockumentary, brainstorm the characteristics of the Pop and Rock music genres. Use these prompts to guide your discussion.

* How does Pop/Rock music sound?
* Which instruments figure strongly in each genre?
* Which performers do you associate with each genre?, e.g. Rock: Foo Fighters, Avril Lavigne
* Who are the fans of each genre?

Now consider the contrasting features of TV documentary and drama. The main features of documentary have been completed in the grid above. See if you can add any more. Then complete the column for TV drama.

TV documentary features	TV drama features
Footage of real events	
Interviews with experts/witnesses	
Presentation of researched facts	

Take elements from the two lists to come up with some features of the hybrid pop/rockumentary.

INTRODUCTION

Insights into a Band

Look carefully at the images on page 101. These come from a rockmentary which followed the Foo Fighters.

Make a list of the different aspects of life on the road and on stage shown in the images.

Now review your list of the characteristics of pop/rockumentaries. How many of these apply to the Foo Fighters example?

Think about how the camera shots and angles and the point-of-view of the narrative is designed to give an 'insider's view' of the tour.

DEVELOPMENT

Preparing a Pitch

Your group has been asked prepare a synopsis for a pop/rockumentary which will be pitched to the BBC.

First agree on the band you will promote.

1 Fooling around on the tour bus

2 On stage during the tour

3 Dave Grohl at the wheel

4 Filming a video diary while on tour

5 Performing on a TV music show

6 Posing for a publicity shot

Discuss how you will use a combination of the elements in the grid below in your 30-minute programme:

Then plan out your synopsis along the lines of the example below.

Programme structure	Mins	On the road footage	Interviews with band	Recorded/Live performance	Interview with director
Establish band/music			Clip of interview with Dave just before the tour		
Introduce (band members)					
Develop selling band/music					
Conclude (Band's USP)					

Prepare your **pitch** to the BBC. Your aim is to persuade the programmers that yours is the best synopsis and so gain the **commission**.

Summarise the strongest points of your programme plan and say how it would appeal to the target audience.

PLENARY

You are the BBC programmers. Listen carefully as each group presents its pitch.

Ask relevant questions about the content and angle of each synopsis

As a class discuss which group's idea is most likely to be commissioned and why.

42 Site and Sound

OBJECTIVES S8, TR8, TW4,

- **To investigate the organisation and conventions of ICT texts, e.g. *CD-ROM, e-mail, web pages***
- **To analyse how media texts influence and are influenced by readers, e.g. *interactive programmes, selection of news items***
- **To choose, use and evaluate a range of presentational devices, on paper and on screen**

Extra Resources

Necessary: Introduction - access to the Internet to conduct a supervised band website search.

In this lesson you will consider the ways in which developments on the Internet have offered opportunities for bands, whether well-known or unknown, to directly address their audiences.

STARTER

Navigating a Site

Consider the webpage shown opposite – the home page for the band, Everise who play in Brighton and Hove. They have been able to promote themselves freely on the Internet by creating their own website.

Examine the navigation buttons on the right-hand side of the screen. Explain what each means and its purpose in attracting visitors to the site.

Share your ideas with the class.

INTRODUCTION

Comparing Sites

With the help of your teacher, conduct a search on the Internet for the website of an internationally-known band, such as U2, Oasis or R.E.M.

Once you have located the website, make notes on the following aspects of the site.

- The layout of the site
- The use of sound and animation
- Opportunities offered for fans to interact with each other

Now analyse the same aspects of the Everise site from its home page opposite.

Discuss how the two sites compare in size and complexity.

DEVELOPMENT

Devising a Home Page

You are going to design a home page for your favourite band.

Agree which of the website features, considered so far, will be included in the home page.

List these ideas and then sketch out your home page. You could use the template on page 103 as a guide.

PLENARY

Display all the finished home page plans.

Each group should choose one plan to comment on. Add a post-it note commenting on one element of the webpage that works well and another note on how one element might be improved.

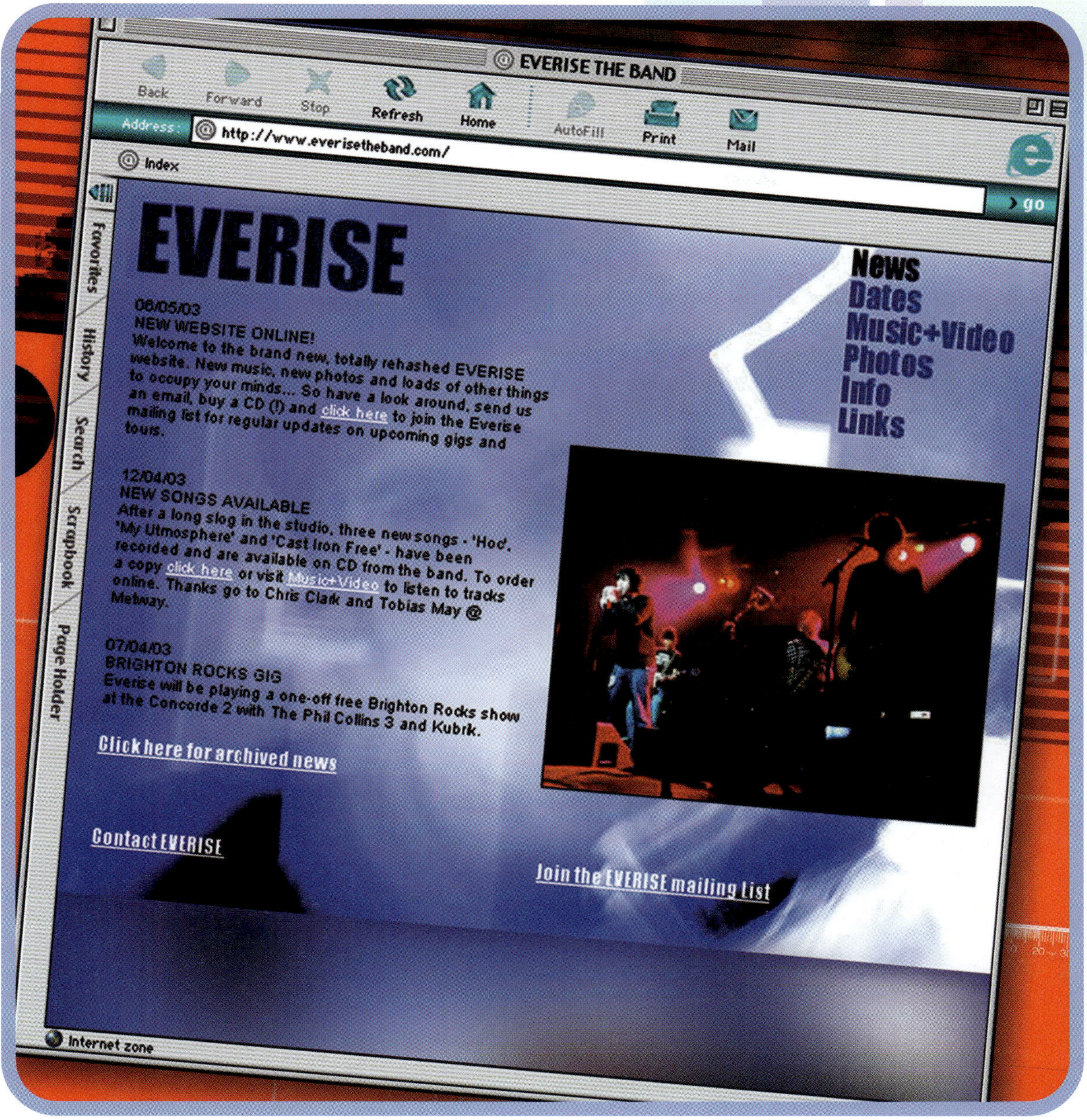

Logo **Website title**		**Search**
Band history: categories – album/ gigs/lyrics	**Video clip/photos on loop**	**Message board**
Fanz update		
Contact us	**Image of band**	
Music	**Welcome to home page message**	
Links		
Help		

43 Copyright – Arguing For

OBJECTIVES W7, TR12, TW2, TW13

- **To recognise layers of meaning in the writer's choice of words, e.g. *connotation, implied meaning, different types or multiple meanings***
- **To analyse and discuss the use made of rhetorical devices in a text**
- **To record, develop and evaluate ideas through writing, e.g. *essays, journals***
- **To present a case persuasively enough to gain the attention and influence a specified group of readers**

Extra Resources

Necessary: Starter – class dictionaries, etymological dictionaries.

In this lesson you will learn about copyright and the way in which people can use copyright to protect what they have created.

STARTER

Copyright Terms

Think about what you understand by 'copying'. Start by brainstorming a list of things that might be copied.

Documents that could be copied

* *Someone's homework*

Now think about the word 'copyright'. Use a dictionary and note down some of the meanings of the word 'right'. Notice that the word can be used as a noun, an adjective or a verb.

Here are some other words that we associate with the copying of people's work such as music or films. Explain what each word means and use an etymological dictionary to discover which language it comes from.

* *Bootleg*
* *Rip-off*
* *Pirate*
* *Download*
* *Burn*

Be ready to share your ideas with the class.

INTRODUCTION

Arguing for Copyright

Imagine you are a successful recording artist with a recent hit single. You discover that copyright has been **infringed** - that there has been widespread copying, selling and downloading of your hit. So you decide to write an article for a music magazine about the harm this is doing to yourself and fellow songwriters.

Drawing on the information in the panels on page 105 and your own ideas, work together on a plan for the arguments you will use to **persuade** readers that copying music is wrong.

Start with a strong statement of the case you are putting forward.

Introduce your arguments in a logical order and support them with evidence.

DEVELOPMENT

Drafting your Article

As a class, draft the first paragraph of your article.

The model below shows one way in which the article might start.

The right to copy seems a 'natural' right for everyone because if something, for example a painting in a museum, exists in the public domain, then I should be able to respond in anyway I like to this. One could say that there is no such thing as an 'original' because all art forms are influenced by other artists. Or is the case a bit more complex?

Now use the rest of the plan to help you write the remainder of the article on your own. Remember you need to offer logical arguments that will **persuade** people not to make bootleg copies.

Incorporate some of the features of good discursive writing listed on page 105 in drafting your argument.

CLA

Why Copyright is Important

Copyright is important because it protects the interests of

those who *create*, and
those who *invest in creativity*.

If there was no copyright, it would be impossible for creative people to make a living from their creativity.

No one would be willing to come up with the large sums of money to make a film, to publish a book, or to bring out a record - because there would be no way of earning a return on that investment.

Now that it is so easy to copy material, it is vital that we respect copyright so that more and more people produce the creative works which the information superhighway must carry if it is to add value to our lives.

Copyright Licensing Agency website

Notice that there are two categories of people who need to be protected, according to the CLA.

Those who create: Copyright exists to ensure that people who create through writing songs, novels, poems, plays or films have a right to any money that is earned through their work. So for example if you write a song, anyone who wants to perform it will have to pay you for the rights to do so. Money is also due to you if it is played on the radio, used in a film soundtrack or as part of a television advertisement. The money you receive for others using your work is called a **royalty**.

Those who invest in creativity: Copyright also exists to ensure that companies which put money into (invest in) the production and promotion of a popular song, for example, will have a chance to make a profit out of the sales of the record. The law argues that if they invest in this way, it would be unfair for someone to come along and copy the song without paying for it. Remember the artist also relies on people willing to invest in their creativity.

Features of discursive writing

- The present tense, e.g. I believe
- Logical connectives, e.g. Some might say, but others... on the other hand, in contrast,
- Lists of three, e.g. it is unacceptable because...reason 1...,...reason 2...,......reason 3...
- Rhetorical devices, e.g. questions 'How can any real music-lover...?'
- Emotive language, e.g. 'this may put at risk...'

Many of these features occur in the model first paragraph on page 104.

PLENARY

Listen to several of the articles that have been written.

Judge whether each puts forward a coherent argument and vote on whether it would stop readers making copies and infringing copyright.

44 Copyright – Arguing Against

OBJECTIVES TW2, TW14. SL2

- To record, develop and evaluate ideas through writing, e.g. *essays, journals*
- To make a counter-argument to a view that has been expressed, addressing weaknesses in the argument and offering alternatives
- To use standard English to explain, explore or justify an idea

In this lesson you will learn more about copyright issues and argue the case against.

INFO

FANS

The noun **fan** derives from the word **fanatic** which means someone who is 'excessively enthusiastic' for example about a religion or a political ideal. It is because of the enthusiasm of their fans that artistes, like Robbie Williams, are asked to sign recording contracts worth many millions of pounds. In contracting established stars record companies gamble on their continuing popularity to make them profits.

STARTER

Fan Power

Fans of an artiste or band fuel their success not only by buying their music but also by purchasing different types of merchandise linked to them.

Brainstorm a list products that fans might buy because they carried a certain star's name. Here are a few examples to start you off:

* Clothes, e.g. t-shirts, caps
* Posters
* Toiletries

Discuss the reasons why fans choose to buy these products when the same product, without the star's name on it, costs less.

INTRODUCTION

Arguing Against

Look back at the article you wrote in unit 43, arguing in favour of copyright protection.

Analyse each paragraph of your article to see if you can find a counter-argument, i.e. in favour of music being free for people to copy. Make notes following the model below.

Point from article: 'Nothing in life is free, so why should downloading tracks from the Internet be?

Counter-argument: Music industry has been exploiting devoted fans for too long – with inflated prices for all music formats – DVD, CD and VHS. Needs to be some trade-off – it should not be illegal to download music from Internet.

It may help to read the article about the Napster software on page 107, where arguments on both sides are put forward.

INFO

NAPSTER

Napster was computer software that enabled music fans to download music free from the Internet. The founder of Napster was sued by the band, Metallica for violating their copyright. Some bands, however, came out in support of the Napster arguing that music should be made free to fans in this way. In fact, it was argued in court that Napster stimulated the sales of CDs, as fans used the service to sample tracks before going out and buying them.

DEVELOPMENT

Structuring the Argument

Imagine you are to take part in a television discussion programme about copyright and the music industry. You have been asked to **argue** the case that the free downloading of music from the Internet is not wrong.

Mom, I blew up the music industry

At 19, Shawn Fanning has a number one haircut, a half-finished degree in computer studies, and is being sued by his favourite band, Metallica. These three facts all contribute to the rather complicated mess Fanning's got himself into, and explain how a nerdy Boston college kid ended up a paper multi-millionaire, an international youth icon, and the centre of a legal storm that will ultimately decide the nature of the music industry's future.

Metallica are suing the company Fanning helped found, Napster Inc, for copyright infringement. This is because of a free piece of software written by Fanning called 'the Napster'. It's simple to download from the Net and makes it easy, for the first time, to get your hands on high-quality copies of chart music for free. Metallica, first among a list of disapproving major artists that includes Elton John, Sean 'Puffy' Combs and Dr Dre, don't like the loss of record sales that this might mean. Conversely, a host of million-selling bands including The Smashing Pumpkins, Hole, The Offspring, Cypress Hill and Limp Bizkit have come out in support of the freedom the Napster grants. A war of words and writs has erupted. And the haircut? Well, that explains how the ridiculous word 'napster' came to be on the lips of media lawyers and music pundits worldwide. ....

....I ask Fanning how he deals with the idea that Napster facilitates the theft of an artist's music. 'I really can't discuss that,' he says, momentarily distracted by a passing girl. 'It has too many legal implications.' How does he feel about the high stakes of the case? What if he loses? 'It's been a good experience. I've worked as hard as I can, and can't be disappointed. I'm getting burnt out on the whole software development thing. I'm thinking of going back to school. Hanging out, chilling.'

Even if Napster loses, Fanning will have achieved something. 'It's a monumental development,' says Andy Greenwald, online editor of Spin magazine. 'The music industry hyperventilated when home-taping surfaced, but Napster is bigger in its scope. Its very nature - the trading of one song at a time - will place an emphasis on singles. In colleges one song tends to make a hot list, sweep the campus, and then be replaced by another the next week. The most positive thing is that it shows absolute passion in music.' As an *LA Times* editorial said, Napster is, 'in its purest form, hard-core Sixties: free love, free music'.

Back in Fanning's office, an e-mail has just arrived about a possible front cover of *Time* magazine. It brings home the scale of what Napster has done and irreversibly will do. And this is something of which Fanning seems both magically and alarmingly unaware.

by Nick Paton Walsh

Take one of the counter-arguments you identified in the Introduction and write notes for the main thrust of your argument. This may mean reordering and editing your original points. The writing frame opposite provides one example of how you might structure your argument. Remember to give evidence to support each point.

Listen as your partner puts forward their argument to you. Note down the main point and counter-arguments that they make. Feed back on how clearly these points were made.

<u>Counter-argument</u>

Key point from article

Counter point 1
Firstly/to begin, it is clear that/one could argue that...

Counter point 2
Secondly/on the other hand/conversely

Counter point 3, etc.

Summary
To conclude/to summarise, I think/propose/suggest...

PLENARY

Reflect on all the arguments you have heard about the free downloading of music from the Internet. Vote on which argument the class feels is the most persuasive – in favour or against copyright.

45 Analysing Radio Ads

OBJECTIVES TR8, TW4, TW9

- **To analyse how media texts influence and are influenced by readers, e.g. *interactive programmes, selection of news items***
- **To choose, use and evaluate a range of presentational devices, on paper and on screen**
- **To integrate diverse information into a coherent and comprehensive account**

Extra Resources

Necessary: Starter – a variety of radio ads from local and national commercial radio stations. Watches with a second hand or timer.

In this lesson you will consider how radio advertisements are constructed in order to communicate with their audience.

STARTER

Vital Ad Stats

Listen to the selection of radio ads that will be played to you. Analyse each one as follows:

- The type of product being advertised
- The company doing the advertising
- How long the advertisement lasts in seconds
- The style of the advert
- What time of day it might be broadcast

Follow the example below:

Product – anti smoking drugs
Name of advertiser – Nicotinelle
Length of ad – 30 seconds
Style of ad – humorous, supportive
Timing of ad: after 6.00 p.m (young people's watershed)

Share your analyses as a class.

INTRODUCTION

Three Types of Sound

Radio advertisements are different from television commercials in that they cannot use pictures. (Radio is a **blind medium**.) Instead, radio advertisements make up for the lack of images by using different types of sound.

Listen to one of the ads again and draw a spider diagram like the one above to show how it uses the three sound elements of radio ads:

- Use of voices
- Use of sound effects (including silence)
- Use of music

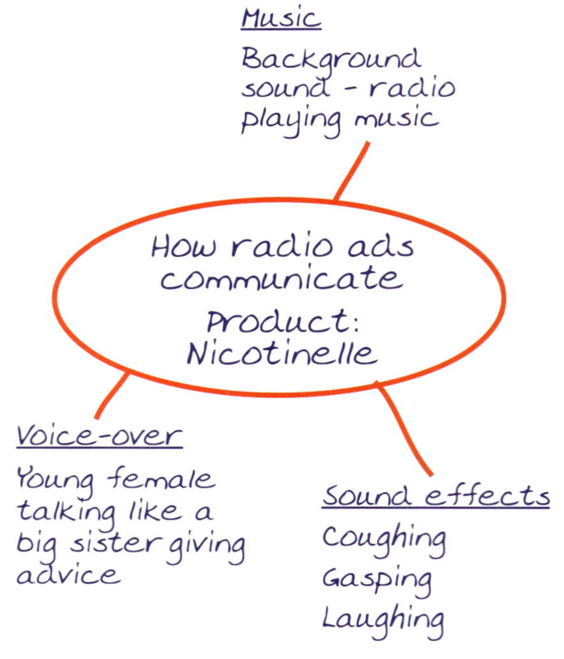

You may need to listen to the ad several times to gather all the information.

Pool your ideas for the different ads with the class.

DEVELOPMENT

Sounds that Persuade

You have already identified the individual sound elements of your chosen ad. Now make notes on how the advertisement uses each item to make an impact on the audience and **persuade** them to buy the product. Use the list of features below to guide you.

- Voices, e.g. dialogue, monologue, voiceover
- Tone of voice used male/female/young /old

- Sound effects, e.g. background noise of car, human sounds (coughing), silence
- Music, e.g. radio jingle/soundtrack
- Other technical effects, e.g. cuts, fade up/fade down, layering of sound (multi-channel editing)
- Language used, e.g. formal/informal, standard English/dialect, slang

Write a commentary on your chosen advertisement analysing how it uses the main conventions of radio ads to address the target audience and **persuade** it to buy the product.

Describe what is being **denoted** and the **connotations** of the script. Give precise examples.

PLENARY

Listen as pairs present to the class a brief example from either their denotation or connotation.

For each example feed back on improvements that might be made to the written explanation or the analysis.

46 Devising a Radio Ad

OBJECTIVES TR8, TW4, TW7

- **To analyse how media texts influence and are influenced by readers, e.g. *interactive programmes, selection of news items***
- **To choose, use and evaluate a range of presentational devices, on paper and on screen**
- **To explore how non-fiction texts can convey information or ideas in amusing or entertaining ways**

Extra Resources

Optional: Starter – taped slogans and catchphrases from ads on local radio.

In this lesson you will devise and script your own radio advertisement.

STARTER

Language of Radio Ads

Working in a small group, write out the handwritten catchphrase below taken from an ad for a Ministry of Sound album.

Now annotate examples in this catchphrase of the following word- or sentence-level language features:

- The imperative
- The superlative
- An acronym
- Slang terms
- A brand name

Use the model as a guide for your annotations.

Use of the superlative

Get the best ever DJ sounds from the ultimate Ministry of Sound Summer remix 2003.

Identify the unique selling point of the product.

Be ready to share your ideas with the class.

INTRODUCTION

Conventions of the Script

Read the script on page 111 which is for an advertisement for Gala Bingo in Brighton.

First analyse the content of the ad, also known as the **sequence**. This often has narrative qualities. (See model on page 111.)

Then consider the conventions in the script which detail the three sound elements included in different parts of the ad. Find examples of:

- Timings
- Settings: OB (outside broadcast) or Studio
- Voiceover/dialogue
- Sound effects
- Music

DEVELOPMENT

Scripting Your Ad

Advertisements on commercial radio stations are often for local businesses. Choose one of the following companies to promote in a 30-second radio ad.

- Ted Barrett's - second-hand car dealers
- *Go Further - travel agency*
- *Wheels R Us* - cycle shop
- ABC Music - musical instrument shop

First plan out the sequence for your advertisement using a grid like the one on page 111. Will the 'story' be delivered by dialogue or by a voice-over? Or will the ad be more informational? Decide which settings will be OB and which studio-based.

Next map out in your script the different types of sound that will go with each stage of the sequence.

Add timings for each stage and the editing effects you might use to blend the stages together, e.g. cuts, fade up/fade down

Use your planning grid to draft the radio ad, following the conventions of the Gala Bingo script above. Remember to use the language features of radio ads identified in the Starter.

When your script is complete rehearse it to check that the timings work within the 30-second limit.

Radio Script from JUICE 107.2, Brighton

Client: Gala Bingo **Duration**: 30 Secs
Ref: 5162 **Executive**: Laurence Elphick
Title: Dream **Writer**: Stewart
D/Req: **On Air**:

SFX: *Dreamy harp sequence*

SFX: *Door shuts*
FVO: Oooooh look at my brand new house…

SFX: *Sports car starts up*
FVO: Oooooh and me new car…

MVO: *(Spanish hunk)* Hello ma leedle princess
FVO: Oooooh and me brand new Spanish boyfriend…
Knowing my luck it'll turn out to be just a dream.

SFX: *Straight away dream goes 'POP'*
FVO: Oh flip it was.

Anncr: *(Enthusiastic)* Turn your dreams into reality at Gala Bingo where we pay out up to a MASSIVE **40 grand** EVERY evening!!
AND IT'S FREE TO JOIN!!!!!
What are you waiting for? – Get down to Gala Bingo, (address)…
And find out why Brighton's Bingo-ing mad!

Timing	Setting	Sequence	Sound effects/music
Time 4 secs	OB	Opens in club V/O: Was your day so bad that you want to go straight to the pub?	fade up Water gurgling Gentle talking fade down
5 secs	OB	Goes into swimming pool V/O: Imagine an oasis of calm waiting for you at any time of the day	fade up Classic music/soft cut to
5 secs	Studio	Aged 25-35 women V/O: Imagine state of the art gym with qualified trainers	Two women talking about classes Soft music

PLENARY

Listen as one pair reads their radio advertisement.

Assess how well they have used:

- The three sound elements available to them
- The conventions of editing and scripting

If time allows, recording some of the ads using sound effect tapes would allow you to develop scripts further.

47 Brand New!

OBJECTIVES TR8, TW6, TW7

- **To analyse how media texts influence and are influenced by readers, e.g. *interactive programmes, selection of news items***
- **To exploit the creative and aesthetic features of language in non-literary texts, e.g. *the use of figurative language or the cadence of sentences***
- **To explore how non-fiction texts can convey information or ideas in amusing or entertaining ways**

In this lesson you will be looking at how language is used to sell products for example in trademarks and slogans.

STARTER

What's in a Logo?

What is a logo? Write a brief definition for this term. Then check it against the definition in the Glossary.

Choose one of the logos or the trademarks on page 113 and note down what it communicates. Be exact in your explanation; refer to the shape of the logo or typeface and to the colours used. Use the example below to guide you.

Nike's Swoosh Design trademark and the 'Just Do It.' trade mark signify a specific attitude to sport and life in general as well as stylish sportswear endorsed by famous celebrities like footballers. When the reader sees the trademarks, all the values for the product are also read and reinforced in the mind of the audience.

Be ready to share your explanations with the class.

INFO

Trademarks

A trademark is a sign which allows a customer to recognise the product of a particular trader. A trademark can include words, logos, pictures or any combination of these. Trademarks are legally registered to help protect the trader's interest in the product.

INFO

Branding

Branding is one way the company marks out the product from any other rivals selling similar products. The brand suggests to the prospective buyer all the highly-desirable qualities that warrant spending money on this product rather than another. For example, named brands are seen to be more appealing than own brands, i.e. products produced directly for the retailer.

INTRODUCTION

Designing a Logo

Now it is your turn to go through the process of designing a logo. Start by selecting a product/company from the list below:

- EcoWash – an ecologically-sound washing powder aimed at the environmentally-minded
- House Mates – a new chain of estate agents, aimed at first-time buyers
- Build-U-Like – a DIY store aimed at homeowners aged 25+
- Range Elle – a new collection of women's clothes aimed at young professional women

Discuss your chosen product and decide whether you will:

- Make the new logo 'relevant' to the work the product/company does
- Or use the logo to emphasise the positive qualities of the product/company

Use the product name to brainstorm ideas for the shape, colour and content of the logo.

Sketch several designs for the logo and agree on which one suits your product and target customers best. Write a short explanation of the **connotations** your logo transmits.

DEVELOPMENT

Creating a Brand

Brand names are very often used in the advertising slogans which are used to sell products, e.g. Beanz meanz Heinz.

Brands become very closely linked to their slogans as well as their logos. How many of the following slogans can you match with their logos above?

Every little helps

You can do it for less at Asda

Brighter Shopping

ideas for life

Just Do It

For moments money can't buy

making life taste better

WELL WORTH IT

Look again at these slogans and identify the types of language they use from the list below:

- Puns/word play
- Alliteration/Assonance
- Similes
- Rhyme

Return to your product and logo from the Introduction. Now come up with a slogan that:

- Reinforces the positive qualities of the your product
- Refers to its unique selling point
- Uses some of the language features above to make it memorable

Write a short explanation of the reasons behind your slogan and how it complements the logo you have created.

PLENARY

Listen as pairs present their product logo and slogan.

Discuss how successful each pair is in using these key forms of promotion.

Give constructive feedback on how logos and slogans might be improved.

48 Letters Eight-Foot High

OBJECTIVES TR8, TW4, TW12

- To analyse how media texts influence and are influenced by readers, e.g. *interactive programmes, selection of news items*
- To choose, use and evaluate a range of presentational devices, on paper and on screen
- To exploit the potential of presentational devices when presenting information on paper or on screen, e.g. *font size, text layout, bullet points, italics*

In this lesson you will look at one of the biggest print texts of all, billboards, and their potential to create impact in an advertising campaign.

INFO

Billboards

Billboards were one of the original ways of advertising a product in towns and cities to a mass audience. They predate all forms of moving image mass marketing such as TV and cinema advertising. New technology allows billboards to revolve, meaning that several adverts can be shown at once in one billboard space.

STARTER

Not as Seen on TV

Make a class list of the different products you have seen advertised on billboards recently.

Consider some of the ways billboards differ from advertisements on television or in a magazine. Focus on:

- The sheer size and type of image that can be displayed
- Language choice and length of text
- Language of slogan
- Other printed information: company name/web address

Feed back your ideas to the class.

Extra Resources

Optional: Starter – photos or OHTs of billboards displayed locally.

INTRODUCTION

Split-second Ads

In a car, bus or train, the time spent viewing a billboard is only a second or two. Almost as soon as we see them on the roadside, they are gone. Yet billboards still make a tremendous impact.

Read the AA billboard on page 115. Discuss how it makes use of following features to achieve impact on the reader:

- Text
- Image
- Slogan
- Colour
- Layout

For example:

AA Billboard

Image: the image dominates the frame and is centred to the right of the text. The image is a close-up to achieve maximum impact on the passing reader. It shows a middle-aged woman...

Be prepared to share your comments with the class.

DEVELOPMENT

Designing your Billboard

Work together to design a billboard, complete with slogan, which will promote of one of the following products:

- Refresh - a new instant coffee, aimed at busy professionals
- Superfly - new 'light-as-air' trainers, aimed at fashion-conscious teenagers
- Shield - new charity for the homeless, aimed at those with disposable income

Refer back to the list of billboard features on page 114 and include the ones that are relevant to your product.

It may help to use one of the billboard templates shown here as a guide for the layout of your billboard.

Template 1

Large title of product	
Image Need to also add here The slogan/shoutline	Product information
Contact details/website	

Template 2

Product information	Image Key words/slogan listed
Contact details/web address	

Finally, decide where, in your local area, a billboard might be sited to have the maximum impact.

PLENARY

Display your designs on the classroom wall like a gallery. Each group should focus on one design and add a post-it to it with one positive comment and one suggestion for improvement.

Use the comments to improve upon your design.

Storyboard Skills

Storyboards are used by people working in film, television and advertising to plan ideas and to show other people how a sequence might look when it has been filmed. A storyboard is a useful shorthand way of getting down ideas about how a sequence might look without the expense of using video or film equipment.

THE MAIN COMPONENTS OF A STORYBOARD ARE:

Camera shot size, e.g. close-up, long shot
Camera directions, e.g. pan, zoom
Dialogue (what the characters say)
Music
Sound effects
Voice-over
Editing features, e.g. cut, fade, dissolve
Timing
Special effects (if appropriate)

A storyboard shows each part of the sequence as an individual **frame** which is drawn to the same proportion as the image that will be seen on the screen (This is called the aspect ratio; an ordinary television screen has an aspect ratio of 4:3.

When you create a storyboard, you need to use each of these frames to provide all the appropriate information about what should happen in that part of the sequence. In the box above there is a list of elements that are generally included for each individual frame.

CAMERA SHOTS AND MOVEMENTS

Probably the most important information to include in a storyboard is about what the camera will be doing when the sequence is filmed. The two key elements of this are:

- Shot size, which means how big people and objects will appear on the screen when the sequence is shown
- Camera movement, which means whether the camera will be still or whether it will be moving in relation to the person or object being filmed

The most important camera shots are:

- **The establishing shot** (ES) This usually comes at the start of a sequence and establishes what is happening, who is involved and where this is taking place. For example, in a news report where a reporter is interviewing someone about a bank robbery, the establishing shot would show the reporter and interviewee standing in front of the bank.
- **The close-up** (CU) This fills the screen with a character's head and shoulders. It is a good shot for showing people's emotions. For example, in a soap opera when someone is crying or upset it is often in close-up.
- **The long shot** (LS) This is used to show a broad view and helps us to see the context that people are set in. For example, a film might open with a long shot showing a town in the distance before moving closer to show us the individuals who live in the town.
- **The mid shot** (MS) – This is used to show detail without being a close-up. For example, in a film a mid-shot might focus closely on one character's actions, showing the top half of their body.
- **The point-of-view shot** (PoV) This shows us the action as though we were seeing it through the eyes of a particular character. For example, in a horror movie the point-of-view shot might be used to show us the action through the eyes of someone who is afraid of something which is hiding in their house.

When planning a storyboard, directions to the camera should also be included. To write these you need to be aware that the camera is able to move in the following ways:

- **Panning** This is probably the most common movement the camera makes. The camera pans when it moves horizontally from one object to another, usually by turning on a tripod.
- **Tracking** This is where the camera is placed on a track like a railway line and moves alongside the action which is taking place.
- **Zooming** This gives the impression that the camera is moving closer to (zooming in) or further away (zooming out) from an object by making the shot size bigger (close-up) or smaller (long shot) on the screen.

EDITING AND TIMING

On your storyboard you also need to say how long each shot will last. Try watching a sequence such as a television advertisement and time how long each shot lasts.

When a sequence changes from one shot to another, you also need to indicate how this change is made, selecting from this range of editing techniques.

- **The cut** This is the most common form of 'edit', where one shot stops and another replaces it straightaway.
- **The dissolve** This is where two shots are overlapped, by fading one into the other.
- **The fade** This is where a shot slowly turns to a blank screen before another shot appears from the blank screen.

SOUNDS WORKING WITH IMAGES

Finally, when planning your storyboard, you will need to think about the way in which different types of sounds will work together with the images to create meaning.

You can indicate the sounds that will be heard by writing this information below each frame.

- **Dialogue** Words spoken by the people on screen
- **Voice-over** Words spoken by off-screen narrator
- **Music**
- **Sound effects**

Now turn to the example storyboard for Flakey's New Banana Cereal on pages 118-119, where you will see many of these techniques in action.

FLAKEY'S NEW BANANA CEREAL

1

3 SECS

(LS) A teenage boy's bedroom with a young lad, Jason, asleep in bed covers pulled over his head

No sound

CUT TO

2

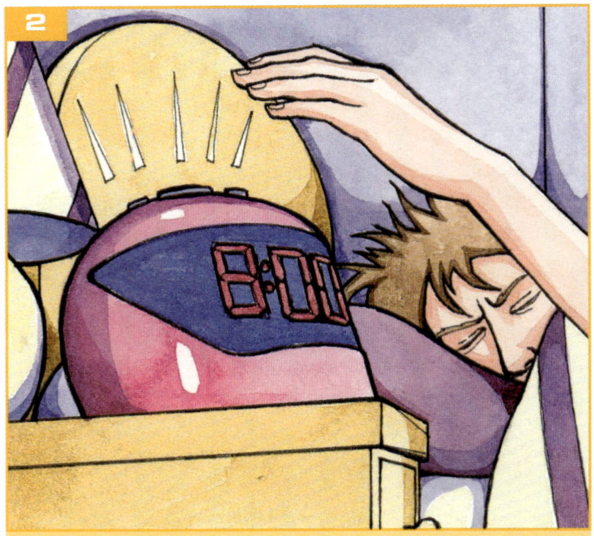

2 SECS

(CU) Jason's alarm clock ringing

CUT TO

3

2 SECS

(LS) Jason's bedroom again

Mother (off screen): 'Come on Jason - time for school.'

CUT TO

4

2 SECS

(CU) Jason with one eye open

Jason: 'Mum, I don't feel well. Can't I stay in bed?'

CUT TO

3 SECS

(LS) From top of stairs showing mother at foot with bowl of cereal in hand

Mother: 'You don't want to try Flakey's New Banana Cereal then?'

CUT TO

2 SECS

(CU) Jason's smiling face

Jason: 'Flakey's New Banana Cereal?'

CUT TO

2 SECS

(LS) Jason leaping our of bed

Jason: 'Feeling better now, Mum.'

DISSOLVE TO

4 SECS

(LS ZOOMS TO MS) Jason eating Flakey's cereal at breakfast table as smug-looking mother smiles knowingly at camera

Camera zooms to a mid-shot of Jason's head, arms and the cereal bowl as he carries on eating

V/O: Flakey's New Banana Cereal - can even get Jason out of bed.

FADE

Glossary

Text in *italics* indicates that the term is defined elsewhere in the glossary.

KEY

M Music
P Print (newpapers and magazines)
R Radio
TV Television and video
F Film
I Internet and electronic communication

Acronym Use of the initial letters of words to represent the organisation, often spoken as a word in its own right, e.g. BARB stands for the Broadcasters' Audience Research Board.

Actuality [R] Sound, recorded or transmitted, of real events that are taking place outside the studio, such as an interview.

Advertising campaign [R TV F] A series of advertisements devised to promote a product via different media over a given period of time.

Angle [P] A particular approach adopted by a journalist to a story.

Animation [F] The method of making drawings or models move on screen, by shooting still images a few frames at a time.

Aspect ratio [TV F] The relationship between the width and height of a TV or film image, e.g. an ordinary television screen has an aspect ratio of 4:3.

Audio [R TV F] Sound.

Autocue [TV] A screen that displays what the presenter has to say during a *Broadcast*.

Big close-up [TV F] A camera shot that shows a face filling a frame, good for expressing strong emotions.

Billboards [P] Large advertising hoardings, often situated at the roadside.

Blind medium [R] A medium that relies purely on sound to communicate with the audience.

Bootleg [M P F] To copy illegally.

Brand name The label by which a product is known, e.g. Heinz or Kelloggs.

Broadcast [R TV] To transmit to an audience.

Broadsheet [P] A newspaper printed on sheets of paper 116.83 x 81.28 cm (46 x 32 inches). See also *Tabloid*.

Bulletin script [R TV] A typed script of the words to be read or which will appear on the *Autocue*, along with other information about the bulletin, e.g. timings for each *Item*.

By-line [P] Information giving the name of the person who wrote a newspaper or magazine article.

CD [M] A compact disc.

Camera angles [TV F] Different ways in which the camera can show action.

Caption [P] Words written under a photograph to explain what is happening.

Catchphrase [P R TV] A memorable and often repeated phrase intended to stick in the mind of the audience. Catchphrases are used in advertisements.

Certificate [F] The classification of a film according to its suitability for different age groups.

Cinema listing [P TV] Details of the films which are being shown at a cinema.

Circulation [P] The number of copies that a newspaper or magazine sells.

Cliff-hanger [R TV] The last dramatic action in an episode of a serial drama that encourages people to tune in to the next episode.

Close-up (CU) [P R TV F] A shot in which only a subject's head and shoulders are shown.

Codes [P R TV F] An element or convention through which the media communicates meaning to us because we have learned how to read it.

Column [P] A long narrow strip of text. Columns are a way of dividing a page vertically.

Commission [R TV] Money is made available by a production company to produce a programme.

Connotation [M P R TV F] The secondary, associated or extra meaning that a *Sign* carries in a addition to its everyday meaning. See also *Denotation*.

Convention [F M P R TV] The accepted or apparently natural way of constructing a media text, which familiarity will have made an audience come to expect.

Copy [P] 1. A story written by a journalist. 2. Words written by an advertising agency to sell a product.

Copyright [P R TV F] Laws designed to protect people from having their ideas and work stolen.

Copyright Licensing Agency [P R TV F] An organisation set up to help protect copyright holders.

Crop [P] To cut down a photographic image, usually to dispose of unwanted detail.

Cut [TV F] An editing technique in which two segments are joined together by simply switching from one to the other.

Denotation [M P R TV F] The primary, everyday or commonsense meaning of a *Sign*. See also *Connotation*.

Digital broadcasting [R TV] A technique of transmitting signals digitally to produce better reception and to allow greater use of capacity by transmitters.

Director [R TV F] The person responsible for the artistic interpretation of a film or programme.

Display advert [P] Large advertisement in newspaper or magazine.

Dissolve [TV F] An editing technique in which one image or scene fades into another.

Docudrama [R TV F] The dramatization of real-life events.

Documentary [R TV F] A media product that is concerned with factual material.

Download [I] To obtain information or entertainment from the *Internet*.

Editing [TV F] The process of putting together a TV programme, advertisement or film from the footage shot.

Editor [P R TV] 1. The person ultimately responsible for the content of a newspaper, magazine or news programme. 2. [F TV] The person who puts together a film or TV programme from the footage shot.

Editorial [P] The content of a magazine that is written by journalists as opposed to that used for advertising.

Emotive language [P R TV F] Words designed to make readers react in a particular way.

Establishing shot (ES) [TV F] A shot that shows the characters in a location, to let the audience know where they are and how they are situated.

Fade [TV F] An editing technique in which an image disappears gradually, leaving the screen blank.

Fade up [TV F] An editing technique in which an image slowly appears from a blank screen.

Feature [P] An article that takes an in-depth look at a topic or issue.

Footage [TV F] Film or videotape that has been shot.

Format [R TV] The way in which a programme is put together or constructed, e.g. a studio discussion.

Frame [TV F] The way the camera is used to place an image within its field of view.

General release [F] When a film is first shown to the general public.

Genre [M P R TV F] The type or category of a film, programme or other media text.

Graphics [P TV F] The use of visual images for illustration.

Grey market [M P R TV F] The potential audience of older or retired people.

Headline [P R TV] The words in large print at the top of an article or spoken at the opening of a news bulletin telling the audience what a story is about.

Home page [I] The opening page of a website that presents the content of the whole site.

Hybrid [M R TV F] A media product that is a combination of two or more *Genres*, e.g. a *Docudrama*.

Image [P TV] A visual representation of something.

Institution [M P R TV F] An organisation that produces media products.

Interactive [TV] Television that allows the audience to interact with the screen, e.g. by calling up additional information or choosing particular camera angles.

Interdependence [M P R TV F I] The way in which different media such as newspapers and television link with one another, e.g. news stories about film, television or music celebrities.

Internet [I] A world-wide system of communication between individuals through the use of personal computers.

Intro [P] The first paragraph of a story.

Item [R TV] A single news story in a bulletin.

Jingle [R TV] A catchy piece of music that helps identify a programme or product.

Juxtaposition [P TV F] The placing together of two things such as words and an image to create meaning

Layout [P] How text and/or images are designed to fit a page.

Leader [P] The main editorial in a *Broadsheet* newspaper.

Link [R TV] Words spoken by a newsreader to connect two news items.

Links [I] Hypertext links which when clicked take you from one webpage to another relevant page.

Live action [TV F] Film or television that involves people as opposed to *Animation*.

Logo [P TV F] A visual image to make a brand recognizable, e.g. the Nike swoosh logo.

Long shot (LS) [TV F] A shot that shows the characters in the distance, with details of their surroundings, before they are seen in *Close-up*.

Main menu [TV I] A list of items from which a viewer or computer user can select.

Market [P R TV F] The potential audience for a media product.

Market research [P R TV] A means of finding out about people's likes, dislikes and lifestyle.

Mass media [P R TV F] Communication to large audiences.

Masthead [P] The title of a newspaper on the front page.

Mid shot (MS) [TV F] A camera shot between *Close-up* and *Long shot* that gives the character and the surroundings roughly equal amounts of the frame.

Multiple narratives [R TV F] Many storylines taking place at the same time.

Multiplex [F] A cinema with many screens.

Napster [M I] Computer software that enabled people to download music freely from the *Internet*.

Narrative sequence The telling of a story or unfolding of a plot that is common to most media texts. It often contains the five stages of narrative: Introduction, Development, Complication, Crisis and Resolution.

Navigation buttons [I] Buttons on a webpage which allow you to move around a particular website.

News [P R TV] Information about what is happening in the world.

News bulletin [R TV] A short summary of the current main news stories.

News reader [R TV] A presenter who announces the news.

News values [P R TV] Factors that influence whether a story will be selected for coverage.

Newsworthiness [P R TV] The quality of information that is considered to be worth publishing or broadcasting.

Niche [P R TV] Media products that appeal to audiences with specific interests.

OB (Outside broadcast) [R TV] A *Broadcast* from outside the studio, usually of an important news or sporting event.

Off-peak [R TV] Less popular viewing times, usually during the day.

On-air [R TV] The time when a station is broadcasting.

On-location [R TV] When a reporter leaves the studio to report from the scene of a news story.

Packaging [M] The way a media product is shaped and promoted, e.g. a band is packaged through newspaper stories and TV appearances.

Pan [TV F] A movement by which the camera moves horizontally from one subject to another or follows a piece of action.

Pilot [R TV] A single programme made to test audience reaction to a possible series.

Pitch [R TV F] To put forward an idea for a programme to a company in the hope that they will *Commission* it.

Point-of-view shot (PoV) [TV F] A camera shot that shows the audience exactly what a particular character sees.

Popumentary [TV] A film that documents the working life of a pop or a rock band through a collection of live performances integrated with interviews and 'exclusive' back-stage footage. It is also a promotional tool.

Press release [P R TV] Publicity material giving information to news media of a forthcoming event, product or programme launch.

Prime time [TV] Peak viewing time, usually the evening.

Product brief [P R TV] Information about a product supplied by the makers to the advertising agency. From this information an *Advertising campaign* will be shaped.

Product launch [P R TV] When a new product is introduced on to the market.

Programming [R TV] Organising the transmission of programmes into a specific order.

Promotion [P R TV I] The marketing of a product through the media, e.g. a band or a perfume.

Ratings [R TV] The number of viewers or listeners that a programme attracts.

Rationale [R TV] The justification for an idea, e.g a new television series. The rationale explains how the programme would work and would appeal to the audience. It convinces a TV company to *Commission* a series.

Readership profile [P] A breakdown of *Market research* data showing the type of people who read a newspaper or magazine.

Register [P R TV F] Language which is appropriate to a specific situation.

Report [P R TV] Details given of what is happening in a news story.

Representation [F M P R TV] The process of communicating by using symbols to stand for things often reflecting a system of values in society, e.g. the way gender or family life is depicted in advertisements.

Review [P R TV F] A critical response to an event or text, such as a film or a novel.

Rhetorical question [P R TV] A question which is asked but which does not require an answer.

Running order [R TV] A sheet that lists each news item in the order in which it will appear in a *Broadcast*.

Satellite broadcasting [TV] The use of satellites to bounce back a signal to earth to be received by a dish.

Schedules [R TV] The organisation of programmes into different *Slots*.

Script [R TV F] Words to be spoken by actors and/or instructions to the film crew.

Script writing [R TV F] The process of creating a script.

Serial drama [R TV] The technical name for a *Soap opera*.

Shoutline [P] A memorable phrase used in advertising that does not usually mention the product or its logo, e.g. 'Get Even' or 'The Power of Dreams'.

Sign [M P R TV F] A word, image or sound that is used to represent an object or idea.

Sitcom [TV] A *Genre* of programme that relies for its comedy on a particular situation, e.g. students living together in a flat.

Slogan [P R TV] A catchy phrase that readers, viewers or listeners will easily remember, e.g. 'Beanz Meanz Heinz'.

Slot [R TV] A time period in TV or radio *Schedules*.

Soap opera [R TV] A *Serial drama* that is usually broadcast several times a week.

Sound effects [R TV E] Additional sounds other than dialogue or music, designed to add atmosphere and realism to a piece.

Special effects [TV F] Use of devices to enhance a moving image text to make it look more exciting, e.g. in science fiction or action films.

Specialist magazines [P] Magazines targetted at readers with specific interests or hobbies.

Stereotyping [P R TV F] Representation of people or groups of people by a few characters. Stereotyping can be negative or positive.

Still [TV F] A static image.

Stock characters [R TV F] Types of character who regularly feature in particular genres.

Storyboard [TV F] A plan of how a sequence will look when it is filmed.

Storyline [R TV F] The plot of a radio/TV drama or of a film. See also *Narrative sequence*.

Sub-editor [P] A person responsible for checking a journalist's copy, deciding on its position in a newspaper or magazine and designing the page on which it will appear.

Submenu [TV I] A menu offering further choices after initial selection from a *Main menu*.

Synopsis [TV F] A short, structured summary.

Tabloid [P] A newspaper half the size of a *Broadsheet*, with pages measuring 58.42 x 40.64 cm (23 x 16 inches).

Talk radio [R] A station which focuses on speech-based output rather than music.

Target audience [P R TV] The particular audience identified through market research as the likely consumers of a media product.

Teaser [P] Information on the cover of a magazine to encourage people to look inside.

Telephone voting [R TV] Calling in to a dedicated phone line to register a choice or opinion.

Teletext [TV] A film and information service broadcast as a separate signal on TV channels, which can be received by a TV set with a special decoder.

Terrestrial television [TV] Television channels whose signals can be transmitted and received only through conventional transmitters and aerials.

Text-message voting [R TV] Texting in to a dedicated line to register a choice or opinion.

Title sequence [TV F] The opening shots of a film or TV programme that tell the audience the title and the stars' names.

Tone [P R TV F] The way in which the audience or the reader is addressed.

Track [TV F] A camera movement along a piece of track which follows action across a horizontal space, e.g. to show a queue of people.

Trademark [P TV] A *Sign* which allows a customer to recognise the product of a particular trader. A trademark can include words, *Logos*, images or any combination of these.

Trailer [F R TV] A highly-edited version of a film or programme designed to interest an audience in the text itself.

Travelogue [R TV] A programme about travel.

TV listings [P TV] Details of programmes that are to be broadcast at specific times.

Two-shot [TV F] A camera shot in which two people are shown in the *Frame*.

Typography [P] 1. The design of lettering in print. 2. The process of typesetting.

Unique selling point [P R TV F] The special aspect of a product that advertisers can highlight in promoting it.

Voice-over [TV F] An off-screen voice that usually tells the story, explains the action or comments on it.

Video diary [TV] An on-going record of a person's thoughts and reactions recorded on videotape.

Visual [P F TV] An image or picture.

Webpage [I] A page of an *Internet* site

Website [I] A publication on the *Internet*, named after the Word Wide Web, which organises the information.

Zoom [TV F] An angle that creates the feeling that a camera is moving towards (zooming in) or away (zooming out) from the subject.

Name: Form:

PC WORDLOG

The grid below will act as a record of the media terms that you will meet in *Channels*.

Add each key term to the left-hand column when you first meet it and then write its meaning in the middle column. You could refer to the Glossary on pages 120-125 to check the meaning.

In the final column add any notes that will help you remember the term or which might help you with the particular activity you are doing.

Media term	Meaning	Notes

© HarperCollins*Publishers* 2003

Name: Form:

PC

SPELLOFAX

Use this grid to help you learn the spellings of the media terms you meet in *Channels*.

Note down the key term in the first column. Then choose one of these spelling strategies to help you remember the right spelling. Write this in the second column.

- Break word down into sounds or syllables, e.g. d-i-a-r-y or ph-o-to
- Split word into affixes, e.g. re-present
- Use a mnemonic, e.g. 'one collar-two sleeves' for necessary
- Refer to a word in the same family, e.g. stereo for stereotype
- Look for words within words, e.g. note in denotation
- Use analogy, e.g. fade/shade/made
- Apply spelling rule, e.g. 'i before e except after c' for special effects
- Learn by sight, use the 'Look, cover, write, check' technique

In the third column, write an example sentence including the word. Check if you get the spelling correct.

Media term spelling	Spelling strategy	Example sentence

© HarperCollins*Publishers* 2003

Acknowledgements

The publishers gratefully acknowledge the following for permission to reproduce copyright material. Whilst every effort has been made to trace copyright holders, this has not proved possible in every case.

TEXT:

p9 © Express Newspapers reproduced with permission; p11 © *The Daily Mirror* reproduced with permission; p11 © Telegraph Group Limited 2002 reproduced with permission; p13 *The Funday Times*, London, 3 February 2003 © *The Sunday Times*/Times Newspapers Limited, London 3 February 2003; p17 courtesy of *TV Quick* 31 January 2003; p21 © Granada Media, reproduced with permission; p28 © Telegraph Group Limited 1998 reproduced with permission; p31 Dy-Na-Mi-Tee Words and Music by Niomi Daley, Salaam Remi, Lennie Hibbert and Clement Dodd © 2002 EMI Music Publishing Ltd, Salaam Remi Music Inc, EMI April Music Inc and Jamrec Music, USA (50%) EMI Music Publishing Ltd, London WC2H 0QY Reproduced by permission of International Music Publications Ltd All Rights Reserved; p35 reproduced by permission of Label at JWT; p39 Samsung A800 advertisement reproduced with kind permission from Samsung Electronics (UK) Ltd, Mobile Division; p40 Boots 17 Cosmetics, reproduced with permission; p41 Sportura watch advertisement reproduced with kind permission of Seiko U.K. Limited; p45 © Hachette Filipacchi (UK) Ltd; p47 *Top of the Pops* magazine reproduced by kind permission of the BBC; p51 extract from *Shout* magazine courtesy D.C.Thomson & Co., Ltd.; p55 Elijah Wood Fan Network page reproduced with permission, http://www.elijah-wood.com/; p59 review of *Wild Thornberrys* Film, Philip French, 9 February 2003, Observer © Philip French; p59 reproduced by kind permission of Teletext Ltd; p63, 65 radio news scripts courtesy of Crawley Newsroom at Mercury FM; p67 Radio 4 *Moral Maze* transcript reproduced by kind permission of the BBC; p71 *The Daughter of the Sea* reproduced with permission, © David Calcutt; p85 (c) HIT Entertainment PLC and Keith Chapman 2003; p87 extract from *My Weekly* courtesy D.C.Thomson & Co. Ltd.; p89 courtesy of *TV Quick*, 25-31 January 2003; p95 *Daily Mail*; p97 article from *Heat* magazine, 15-21 February 2003, reprinted with permission; p99 *What's On TV* articles used with permission of the publishers, IPC media; p103 website courtesy of Everise, www.everisetheband.com; p105 The Copyright Licensing Agency Ltd, www.cla.co.uk; p107 *Mom I blew up the Music Industry*, Nick Paton Walsh 21 May 2000 *Observer* © OBSERVER; p111 courtesy of Juice 107.2 FM, © Forever Broadcasting; p113 The NIKE name, Swoosh Design mark and "Just Do It" are trademarks of Nike, Inc. and its affiliates. Used by permission; p113 reproduced with the permission of The Boots Company PLC; reproduced by kind permission of Sainsbury's Supermarkets Ltd, Tesco Ltd, The Early Learning Centre, Woolworths Plc, Argos and Asda; p115 reproduced courtesy of the Automobile Association.

PICTURES:

p13 AFP/Francis Tenman and UNP Ltd; p19 BBC Photo Library; p21 © Granada Media, reproduced with permission; p23 © BBC Photo Library; p25 © Redferns Music Picture Library reproduced with permission; p27 © Rex Features Ltd reproduced with permission; p28 © PA Photos Limited; p31© Rex Features Ltd reproduced with permission; p33 Blue Pig Design Company; p43 © Zhenya Matysiak; p57 courtesy of LUCASFILM LTD. *Star Wars: Episode II - Attack of the Clones* (C) 2002 Lucasfilm Ltd. & TM. All rights reserved. Used under authorization. Unauthorized duplication is a violation of applicable law; p71 © Zhenya Matysiak; p73Nestlé UK; p75 Lynx Pulse reproduced courtesy of BBH; p77 the Kellogg's Frosties storyboard is reproduced by permission of Kellogg Company; p79 © Zhenya Matysiak; p81 *Jellikins* reproduced courtesy of Toontastic Publishing Ltd; p88 © Janek Matysiak; p89 courtesy of Yorkshire Television Ltd.; p91 *Samurai Jack* and all related characters and elements are trademarks of and © Cartoon Network. An AOL Time Warner Company. All Rights Reserved; p93 © BBC Photo Library; p95 London Features International Ltd; p95 Kudospix; p97 © PA Photos Ltd; p101 Foo Fighters © Mick Hutson/Redferns; Martin Philboy; Stockpop.com/Redferns; p109 © Zhenya Matysiak.

Answer to Introduction activity on page 64
The correct order of the paragraphs in the 'Madonna in Miniature' article is: C, G, E, B, H, A, D, F.